Lazy Happy Successful

An easier path to a happier life

Working hard is the new stupid

About The Author

David Leon is an acclaimed international speaker and successful entrepreneur who has had the privilege to be invited to speak on stages around the world with the likes of Sir Richard Branson, Anthony Robbins, Robert Kiyosaki and many more. His passionate zest for life and his no nonsense content delivery make him a very sought after speaker and commentator. The successes from his clients is living proof that his unconventional ideas and strategies work.

Copyright © David Leon 2022

The right of David Leon to be identified as Author of this work has been asserted by him in accordance with the Moral Rights Act.

All rights reserved. No part of this book may be reproduced or transmitted by any person or entity (including Google, Amazon or similar organisations), in any form or by any means, electronic or mechanical, including photocopying, recording, scanning or by any information storage and retrieval system, without prior permission in writing from the publisher.

Special Dedication

This book is dedicated to all my family members, friends, teachers, colleagues and other random people who tried to put me down by calling me lazy. Thanks to your constant reaffirming, I have become the happy success that I am today.

Preface

Having had the opportunity to coach through my businesses thousands of people in the art of creating wealth and happiness, I have been able to observe first hand that there is very little correlation between hard work and success. I have presented my strategies and ideas in 8 different countries to hundreds of thousands of people having being invited to speak alongside some of the most respected success stories of our generation (Sir Richard Branson, Tony Robbins, Robert Kiyosaki, Russ Whitney, Grant Cardone, Gary Vaynerchuck, Tom Bilyeu, etc...) and my observations are shared by most of my peers.

Success and happiness have very little to do with your work capacity and all to do with your thought processes and ability to adapt to your environment. This book's objective is to make you look at life differently whilst becoming more adaptable so you too can hopefully find what so many people look for and fail to find... happiness, the true and only measure of success.

Contents

Preface 6
Introduction To The Lazy World - MUST READ 1
Chapter 0 - The Big, Big Lie 6
    Before we even start…. 6
    The Lie 6
    The Science behind my theory 9
Chapter I - Workaholics Are Like Meth Addicts 12
    Meeting The Very Special Douchee 13
    The Workaholic's Sick Nature 17
    Spain is different 18
    Re-organising your priorities 20
    Our flawed school system 21
    The Triple A Principle 24
Chapter II - Live Like A Kid 26
    My Phone Call With Douchee 27
    What If I love what I do for a living? 31
    My Grandad Is Still A Kid 35
    Kids Teach Us How To Relearn Life 36
Chapter III - Redefine Your EGO 39
    Douchee's Weekend Event 41
    You Don't Own Shit! 47
    Why You Must Redefine your Ego 50
    Top 7 Thoughts To Let Go Of To Redefine Your Ego 52

Chapter IV - Be The Dumbest Person In Your Tribe 56
    Douchee's Tribe 57
    Success And Happiness Live In Your TRIBE 67
    The Fire Snake 70
    Online networking is NOT working... 71
    The Importance Of Fun Friends 72
    Moving On Is Not Hard, It Is Healthy 73

Chapter V - Lazy Successes Need Better Systems.................... 76
    Douchee's Office Rendezvous 79
    Time Is Your Only Currency 87
    Question Everything And Then Question It Again 88
    Your Priorities Are Your Starting Point.................................. 90

Chapter VI - Chilled By Nature Successful By Default........... 92
    Was I A Douchee?... 94
    Energy And Flow 100
    Expectations Versus Affirmations 102
    Stress And Health.. 106

Chapter VII - What Are You Good At?.................................... 109
    A Douchee In Bali 111
    Your Personality Traits 121
    Setting Achievable Expectations... 125
    TAG - Think, Act, Get 128
    Male And Female Energy 130

Chapter VIII- Know When To Give Up, You Are Not Rocky Balboa!.. 134
    Douchee Bragg Was Just A DoucheBag................................ 135
    The Square And The Triangle 143
    Not All Quitting Is The Same 144
    There Is No Shame In Quitting 146

The Retirement Fallacy 147
Chapter IX - The Secret: It Is All About Timing 151
    Life Without Douchee 153
    Can You Feel It? 155
    Sympathetic Resonance 158
    Is Timing Cyclical? 159
Bonus Chapters 162
Lazy ideas for positive change 162
Lazy health 168
    Sleep can make you healthier and even lose weight! 168
    Managing your weight. The obesity epidemic problem 169
    My favourite Lazy health trick 171
    Maximise your hormonal cycle 174
    Stop eating SHIT 177
Lazy money 180
    The 4 lane motorway to passive wealth 181
    Hormonal cycles affect your investment decisions 188
    Always a learner 190
    Understanding ROI and ROTI 190

Introduction To The Lazy World - MUST READ

We have been sold a noxious idea that happiness lives at the end of your goals, at the highest point of success, at the realisation of your untapped potential; and this idea is quickly crippling people and creating the biggest mental health pandemic that humanity has ever seen. We have bought the idea that to be happy we need to be uber-successful financially. We also need to have the perfect relationship, family, friends and a toned-up body to go with it; and of course, this is all worthless unless you flaunt it all over social media. The most interesting fact about this idea is that those people flaunting their perfect life are just as unhappy if not more as the ones looking at the pics and videos and wishing they were in their shoes. You see, getting somewhere is not what will make your life better or worse, it is the enjoyment of this journey that we call life that will make you happy and based on my definition, a true success story.

Enjoying every step of the journey means exactly that and not what motivational speakers have preached for the last couple of decades. It means that you accept reality and deal with it positively.

Introduction To The Lazy World

What I am talking about and infuriates me is the concept of denial and wishful thinking that these charlatans peddle. The preposterous idea is that you can create reality by just changing your mindset. Well, guess what, you can't! Denial (pronounce "The Nile") is not just a river in Egypt. You can't trick your subconscious into being someone that you are not or into liking things that you truly and deep down don't enjoy or want to do. You can fake it or hide it for a while but I can assure you that it will come back to haunt you and the effects are clearly visible in today's broken society. Using techniques like NLP (Neuro-Linguistic Programming), self-hypnosis and affirmations only mask the real problem. The real problem is that you are being someone and doing something that goes against your true nature and when you do things that don't fit with who you are, the result is almost inevitably always the same: failure and pain, lots of pain. The biggest issue with this problem is that it tends to create a repetitive pattern of failure and pain. Let me explain this concept because it is a fairly important one and clearly affects today's unhappy world. The more you fail, the more likely you are to make failure part of your programming and your self-image and replicate it in future endeavours. This is why I cringe when self-help gurus tell people to go out there and fail as many times as they can and just make it into a learning experience.

These "gurus" will also say there is no failure, only feedback. Yeah right! Adding connotations to a word only masks its true meaning. For example, you can say that a dog is a big cat as much as you want and try to convince yourself that the new meaning and assessment of what you used to know as a dog is now a big cat but at the end of the day it is still a fucking dog!

A string of failures takes its toll on your opinion of who you are and that will in return create more of the same results whether you call those results failures or learning experiences.

My philosophy is pretty simple and it works, STOP FAILING!!! Easy for you to say, you may be thinking…. well, it is not as complicated as you may think it is. The key is pretty simple: think better. Think, think, think. Only when you think enough shall you act in a way that will lead to a fulfilled life. Napoleon Hill titled his best-selling book, which I still consider to be the best self-help title ever written, "THINK and grow rich". It is by improving the quality of our thinking that we create better answers and solutions that will create a happier and ultimately better life. I will attempt to decipher and clarify some of these thoughts in the next few chapters so you can create your new happy paradigm by doing some more introspective thinking.

I love to have fun and I believe this to be true for most humans. I make a point of making my life as much fun as possible because I know it is what makes me vibrate and perform at a higher level. I can almost certainly associate the most successful and happy times of my life with the times I was having more fun. This book will not be any different and I hope to make it more enjoyable and

Introduction To The Lazy World

memorable by making you smile and even laugh with some of my stories and even by using some colourful language. This is why you will meet and hopefully learn to love, Douchee Bragg, our fictional character (although based on my own experiences and people I met and worked with in the personal development industry) who will entertain us and offer a more human and practical angle into the theoretical learning and thoughts I will be trying to expose in this book. Our new anti-hero, Douchee, is a bit of a douchebag. He epitomises everything that is wrong with personal development gurus and to be honest a lot of his attributes are based on my sporadic acts of douchebaggery, not just all of the douchebaggery (and there is a lot of it) that I get to see and experience first hand in the industry. When you get to speak for thousands of hours on stages all over the world you end up catching yourself saying and doing some very douchebaggy things. Saying that, I am an entry-level douche, and I barely make a splash into the douchebaggery currently on show in the industry which still baffles me even after almost two decades fully immersed in it. Please don't get me wrong, not all speakers are douchebags and the industry is actually doing a lot of good to a lot of people.

You will get a dosage of the Douchee Bragg in every chapter and I am pretty sure you will end up loving him, his cliche teachings and all his steaming bullshit. Don't get me wrong, Douchee is a good guy with good intentions but he bases his life on regurgitating cliches and old ideas and strategies that just don't make people happy. Douchee is the equivalent of Deadpool in the Marvel universe. He is a funny, conflicted, good guy who makes some really bad decisions.

So get ready for a different kind of ride. A comfortable and fun ride that will only lead you to positive change by doing less instead of working your ass off. If you open your mind to it and appreciate its simple yet powerful meaning I can assure you that your future will be much brighter. Less is more, life is beautiful, and happiness is success.

Chapter 0 –
The Big, Big Lie

Before we even start....

The lazy happy successful philosophy can't work unless we define what happiness and success mean to you. To me it is pretty simple, being happy is being successful, not the other way around; and being happy means doing more of the things that make my heart sing and elevate my mood and vibration to that level that makes me wanna scream from the rooftops at the top of my lungs how much you love your life.

The Lie

As we grow up we are told a pretty big, fat lie: you need to grow up and behave like an adult. This behaviour typically means giving up the things that made you happy in your previous life to get the things you supposedly need to be happy in this new adult life. Well, I call bullshit on this. The happiest and more successful people that I have met in my life never dropped any of the things that made them happy before adulthood, they just made those things bigger and even more fun! I had the privilege of sharing the stage with the great Sir Richard Branson, a man that epitomises this concept. His constant cheeky smile is a trademark of his lifestyle and success. He has built an empire while having a blast and doing the things he loves doing, like going into space just for kicks and giggles. If you have not read the book "Losing My Virginity" I highly recommend that you do to fully understand this cornerstone of my lazy happy successful philosophy.

On the other hand, I have also shared the stage and met some of the wealthiest and most powerful people in the world who lacked that cheeky smile and zest for life. Meeting them showed me what I do not want my life to be like. Greed and power-hungry "adults" who have no time for play or for all the other things that used to make them happy. Their only source of happiness is their next big deal and telling others about it so they can fill that emptiness that is eating them alive. You can instantly feel their imbalance and subtle but evident frustration about the life they are now living. Money is not what will make you happy but lack of it will hinder your options and opportunities to do the things that will in turn make your life great. But money is a byproduct of your actions, thoughts and energy so unless you dramatically change those actions, thoughts and energy money will always be a problem for you.

I have been teaching people how to make more money for the last two decades. To be exact I have been doing this since 2002.

The Big, Big Lie

Financial freedom is the name of the game for me and that is what I focus a lot of my strategies on. It is not about greed and senseless accumulation of cash and assets; it is about getting your time back so you can use it to do the things that you truly want to do. The biggest issue that people need to overcome when they attend one of my events is that they have forgotten what used to make them happy. Adulthood has taken over and got them spinning that hamster wheel at full pace and getting nowhere fast. They are so occupied doing things that they forgot why they do them to start with. Work has become their life and play and fun have left the building. Getting them to reconnect with their happiness is one of the hardest yet more fulfilling moments of my events. It is challenging for people and I need to push buttons that make people very uncomfortable but in the end, it is worth it. I love being able to be the catalyst for positive change, it is one of the biggest joys of my life.

So before you dive deep into the philosophy that is sure to make your life happier I challenge you to look deep inside yourself and bring up a list of the things that truly make you happy. I don't want you to just think about it, I truly believe that writing them down is essential because that list will help you make better decisions for the rest of your life. For example, if you love surfing more than anything else in your life, don't take a better-paying job inland. It is common sense but common sense these days is anything but common. Here is a list of things to get your juices flowing and help you create your own. Make it pretty and keep it in a handy place because you will use it to make better decisions.

Example: My Happy List:

- Travelling to new places and fully immersing into the local culture.
- Spending more time with my family.
- Listening to music to elevate and/or change my feelings.
- Giving back through my favourite charity
- Playing my favourite sport
- Watching classic movies
- Going for walks in nature
- Playing the guitar
- Gardening

You get the idea, now stop reading this beautiful work of art and create your list. Do not move on until you write it down.

The Science behind my theory

Margaret Mead in her book "Sex and temperament in three primitive societies" which studies several tribes in New Guinea, relates how the Arapesh tribe is mainly a chilled-out tribe of nice, happy, peace-loving people. They live by the ocean, although they often struggle to get enough food for all but still seem to be happy about their environment and their paradigm; this contrasts with the Mundugumor tribe which values trade and social standing and suffers most of its casualties from external wars and internal conflict within family units. Her observations showed that Arapesh children grew up to be content and emotionally levelled individuals while Mundugumor children grew up to be strong but hostile individuals who put their individual success ahead of the tribe's success. This fantastic book is a real eye-opener about human nature and I recommend you read it as soon as you can.

I believe that today's society is a modern interpretation of the Mundugumor tribe. A success-driven society that does not care about global well-being but only about individual competitive "success". This means that people will work beyond their limits and face inhuman levels of stress just to win and become a success at the expense of everyone else. What I will try to break down in this book is how this affects our everyday life and how we can live more like Arapesh in a Mundugumor society.

Dr Stephen Ilardi, who specialises in ethology and the treatment of depression, calls depression a disease caused by our high stressed, industrialised way of live. Depression is now considered an epidemic that takes well over one million lives every year and causes unquantifiable levels of suffering. We now know that it is mainly caused because of our choice as a society to put incredibly high and persistent levels of stress that we are just not capable of dealing with. If we were to control and adjust our stress levels we would dramatically decrease the epidemic that is only getting worse. We can make the world a better place by actually doing less and living more. By going back to our human roots and letting go of our unhealthy pursuit of individual "success". Isn't that a revolutionary concept, it is a logical one! Let's explore it further then…

Chapter I –
Workaholics Are Like Meth Addicts

We are not designed to be workaholics. We can't perform 40+ hours of weekly work, take care of our homes, and loved ones and contribute to society. Just like the lions in the African plains don't hunt for ten hours a day neither should we work our butts off just because society teaches us to do so. Achieving high levels of success does not make us happier, quite the opposite really, they make us miserable assholes. Think about it, in today's competitive society, to reach a high level of success in any field you will need to neglect some other aspects of your life, that is a fact. Balance does not exist in excellence. Any person that achieves a high level of excellence does so at the cost of one or several aspects of their lives and that unbalance creates unhappiness.

A high-performance, driven life is no different to any other addiction. You will do ANYTHING to get to the next level of success that will shoot the next hit of dopamine into your addicted body. When you get there, you feel good for a very short time and then once again you are on the hunt to get the next hit. So stop acting like a crack hoe and get some help to start your bullshit-success detox! This book will show you what real happiness and success look like but in reality, you already know that you just need to rediscover it.

Meeting The Very Special Douchee

I wasn't happy. I was desperately looking for a way out of the constant rat race that my life had become. A recently failed 4 year-long relationship, my bulging waste line and my "successful" business that required me to work ridiculous hours had beaten me to the ground. The debilitating agony my life had become had to stop somehow, and it led me here, to a crowded event sitting next to complete strangers who seemed to be just as pissed off and disappointed with their lives as I was. It was a full-day event with several speakers that promised to change your life. Some of them were hugely recognisable celebrities and some of them weren't, but they all were introduced as superstars and each individual received thunderous standing ovations from the crowd at the packed event as soon as they stepped onto the large and spotlighted stage. The stage was adorned with flowers and massive screens that displayed the speakers and seminar promoters' branding, slides, pictures and videos. It was a well prepared and organised show that resembled more of a concert than a personal development event.

Workaholics Are Like Meth Addicts

After my initial hesitation about the cult-like atmosphere inside the room, I decided to get over my concerns and try to make the most out of the very interesting and valuable information that was to be imparted by the charismatic set of varied speakers. Every speaker had their client testimonials and team members and they were giving out not just their stories but a lot of very valuable information and tips. But just before lunch, one of the speakers completely mesmerised me. I had never heard of him before but his introduction video depicted him as one of the most recognisable figures in the world with his sign-written private plane and having worked and partied with about every celebrity on the planet. His video also showed his charitable work and business feats which looked and sounded spectacular. He started his presentation with one of those mesmerisingly powerful yet slightly annoying American accents which seemed to soften as he kept delivering information. His 90 minute presentation was a parade of ever-growing feats and achievements tied up with pictures with celebrities and luxury items. He even had live customer examples and video testimonials of people that seemed to be doing extremely well after working with him. He called himself the world's number one performance coach and he said so without a hint of hesitation or doubt. His ego was so large that it could easily fill several auditoriums not just our packed and by this stage very energised arena; with a name like Douchee Bragg (pronounced / Doo - Sha /) he definitely needed it… seriously, what a ridiculous name! A couple of guys sitting one row behind me couldn't stop giggling throughout his presentation calling him a whole array of different insulting names. "Mr Douchebag", and "Sir Braggalot", which even I found funny, but the majority of the audience were in a trance-like state fixated on every word that came out of Douchee's mouth. He was mysterious and kind of a walking and talking contradiction. His narcissistic ego was softened by his stories about helping his clients and his selfless charitable work and contributions to the broader community. His energetic on stage persona didn't match his awkwardly contoured and slightly out of shape body. His expensive looking suit and ridiculously bright red tie were not nicely fitted and looked strangely odd on him. He was just right and wrong at the same time and for some reason that I could not pinpoint, I was hooked on the message and especially on the messenger.

Deep down I knew my life wasn't horrible when compared to most people out there. I knew that I was just not happy and that I was quickly digging deeper into that unhappy hole. I just couldn't pinpoint exactly what was creating this discomfort but I knew I needed change and even after just a few minutes, I knew that Douchee was someone that I felt could induce change in me like he had done for so many of his clients. I also knew I was getting sold something throughout his presentation. He even told us within the first 2 minutes of his speech that we would be buying his services because he was the best speaker at the event and offered more value than anyone else. I also knew basically from the moment he started

Workaholics Are Like Meth Addicts

speaking that I was going to buy whatever he was selling. I wasn't wealthy or had huge savings but I knew I needed this and I would spend large if I needed to. About an hour into his speech he told us that if we wanted to change, if we wanted to live the life of our dreams, we had to get off our "ass-ets" and run to the back of the room to sign up for his program. I don't recall exactly what happened next but I remember a blonde middle-aged lady sitting in front of me jumping off her seat and running towards the back of the room. All of a sudden it felt like I was in the middle of a stampede, and there I was, pushing people out of the way to make it to the sales tables at the back of the auditorium before anyone else so I could get my "early action taker bonus gift". I got in supposedly just in time to get the extra value which was a one on one phone call with the man himself, Douchee Bragg.

I got a few manuals and access to his online video library and resources which I was supposed to go through before I had my one on one with him. I parted with a couple of grand but it did not bother me in the slightest. I felt that it was the right choice and that I would easily gain more value than what I paid for his course. I was so enthused and pumped about my decision that I decided to leave the event a couple of hours after I signed up because there was no real point to be there. I already got what I came there to get and I couldn't even concentrate on any of the other speaker's content. I was part of team Douchee!

The Workaholic's Sick Nature

Sebastian Junger in his bestselling book "Tribe", which in my humble opinion is a must-read for anyone wanting to truly understand human nature, describes how early American settlers would often choose to join Native Americans tribes and their way of living while the opposite was very rare. Native Americans that were raised in western ways would often escape and return to their old ways. Mr Junger clearly and extensively explains some of the reasons that may have led to this behaviour, citing a more egalitarian culture and a freer and more in tune with the nature way of living. The fact of the matter is that people chose to leave their culture and join the Native American ones because they were happier there. People need time to disconnect and be in touch with nature, I believe this to be self-evident. We all need to cultivate and nourish meaningful personal relationships and not base our sense of joy on what we achieve or posses. Native Americans didn't accumulate possessions and they shared their hunting spoils equally so they would all have more time to dedicate to leisure activities. This is what creates a higher level of happiness among humans, sharing leisure activities with other people in our circle. Laziness is engraved in our DNA and we are willing to leave everything, including our culture, to pursue it when we find it. This is the reason why cults and gangs have so much appeal to unhappy people. They try to replicate this lifestyle but usually with a sinister and unhealthy undertone.

This is not just true for the Native American cultures but for most indigenous cultures around the world. The western culture took over their way of living but I truly believe that we should have adopted quite a bit of their ways. It is also my opinion that we will see a revival of these cultures in the coming years as people start realising that they are just not happy and that there is a better way.

Spain is different

Coming from Spain, I can personally attest we are the world's masters at creating and using time for leisure. We do leisure better than most people on the planet and to me, this is one of the reasons why Spaniards have one of the highest life expectancy rates in the world (consistently in the top 3) and are some of the happiest people on earth (according to the Eurostat happiness survey, Spain boasts the highest percentage of people who claim to be happy all the time at 29%). Getting together to enjoy a good game of football, to sing, to dance, to have a great long 4 course long lunch; or even just a few tapas and sherries is what we live for. We don't live to work, we work to live. This is what makes Spain a great place to visit and not so good when it comes to financial success or achievement. Obviously, there are always exceptions to the rule as we boast one of the world's wealthiest individuals in Spain in the figure of Amancio Ortega, founder of the fashion empire Zara, but this doesn't make my point any more valid as the leisure-driven Spanish mentality can be observed for hundreds of years even in literary novels like Don Quixote and The Life of Lazarillo De Tormes. These novels portray the cheeky, let's get away with doing as little as possible so we can have fun way of life Spaniards boast. And I want to make this abundantly clear: there is nothing wrong with that! Some of the happiest people I have met live by those principles. On the other hand, constant strife for achievement tends to only lead to constant pain. It is just logical to think that if we are living our life with the primordial objective to achieve something there are only two possible outcomes:

    You achieve that something and then you look for something else. Leads to new pain.

    You don't achieve it and keep trying. Leads to constant pain.

Achievement and evolution will always take place, as it is part of our humanity to push boundaries. The real issue we have to deal with is the obsession this chase of achievement creates. You should be obsessed with your pursuit of happiness, not your pursuit of achievement. Achievement will only be meaningful when you are happy. Achievement without happiness feels empty. The constant pursuit of achievement leads to a workaholic culture, drunk on their futile pursuit of goals having lost perspective on what truly is meaningful for humans. This workaholic culture is predicated upon that next goal, that next drink, that next relationship... it is all the same, just an addiction. And they will do anything to get their next hit. They are willing to sacrifice their lives, their loved ones, their everything, just to have that next hit, that next goal, that next achievement. What I can assure you is that the achievements that you get in your life will look pretty pathetic when you are in your last moments on earth. You will regret not having lived a life pursuing happiness and you will wish you could exchange all your accolades for more happy moments.

Re-organising your priorities

We all get the same number of hours in a day, so it is what you do with them that will determine your happiness and therefore your success. Our indoctrination into our occupation demands that we make our job our top priority. Work and financial success should always supersede all other aspects of your life. Your love life, your friendships, your health, fun and leisure activities should never be above your financial success. The problem with that view is that we end up giving up the best years of our life to our careers while we neglect relationships, health and fun. It is usually too late when we realise that we would be happy to give up all our financial and career success to have the relationships and health to enjoy good, fun, happy times.

I am not saying that your financial situation is not important, quite the opposite. I am saying that you need to modify your priority list to include other aspects of your life and getting the balance right will give you more joy and happiness than you ever dreamed of. Essentially, stop being a stuck-up moron working your butt off to buy shit to impress people that don't even give a crap about you. Start reconnecting with what makes you feel full of life and what makes you smile when you wake up every morning. Your financial situation and success are important because if you play it well, it will leave you more time to do the things you truly want to do. Since this is one of my strengths I have decided to add an extra chapter at the end of this book with some lazy money strategies so you can accomplish your financial goals and more importantly regain your time and freedom. Money will not make you happy, but lack of it will limit your possibilities under our current financial system. Learn to play the game so you can win the game of your life.

Our flawed school system

I have to make a pretty strong and sobering point here. I believe our schools are doing a fucking terrible job of preparing our kids to live a happy and successful life. The obsolete way we are approaching our education is creating a young generation that is unhappy and full of mental and physical health issues.

The worst thing about our educational system is that what we are teaching is completely irrelevant because of our current technological advances. Memorising and regurgitating data is almost completely useless in a world where your phone can process gigantic amounts of data in milliseconds. Instead of focusing on facts, our educational system should focus on creativity, leadership, communication and especially on the achievement of happiness.

Workaholics Are Like Meth Addicts

We are instead creating a generation of useless, stressed, mentally and physically sick people. And we are doing this for one simple reason, to feed our financial system. Our economy demands growth. It needs progress and production to keep growing, anything else means failure and that can't be tolerated because capitalism would topple. We started implementing these measures for increased productivity and performance during the industrial revolution. The information age brought us to hope that we could get some of our recently stolen time back thanks to the advancements in technology like the use of emails and the internet. Unfortunately, these advancements just led to a more connected life with even less available time for leisure and the pursuit of happiness. The trend unfortunately seems to continue and we are now almost physically attached to our mobile phones. We have become slaves to social media and constant notifications.

We live in a stressed-out society where idiots congratulate and admire even bigger idiots who are sacrificing their most valuable asset, their time, just to achieve high levels of financial and business success. Talk about the blind leading the blind…. These people who have given up their lives to achieve high levels of financial and business success are revered as demigods. Well, I have met a fair few of them and in most cases, they are not that happy or even that special. Stop putting these artists, celebrities, entrepreneurs and athletes on a pedestal because they truly don't belong there. That pedestal is just a socially constructed evil fuckup built and designed to get idiots to work as hard as humanly possible in the dreaded hamster wheel.

But I don't do blaming well, it is not in my nature. I like to take responsibility and look at solutions instead. As parents, we are responsible for what happens to our kids and we have no right to blame our fucked up school system and wash our hands of any blame. Since you now know that our school system is just going to create a messed up adult, it is up to you to give your kids what they need to become happy adults who can in turn produce an even happier and better future generation. The best way to show your kids a better way to live life is for you to start living your life in a better way. Isn't that a bloody beautiful sentence! Kids will call your hypocritical bullshit and you will quickly lose their respect. So, if you want to make a difference, and I know you do because you are not a psychopath, make sure you show your kids what their priorities should be. That means that work doesn't come first and your fucking slave driver of a phone stays silent most of the time. Your work stress does not make it into your home and if it does you are quick to apologise and make fun of your temporary insanity. Laugh, have fun and bloody play! Unlearn the messed up programming that you were sold in school and the movies. Life is not that complicated, we have just decided to make it so. Simplify the shit out of it and lead by example as you do so.

The Triple A Principle

I have found that most people struggle to make decisions. Life and decision-making are not that complicated. I designed the Triple A Principle to simplify the decision-making process and clearly explain it to my clients during my events. I usually explain it as it relates to wealth or actually lack of wealth, but it can be transferred to any other decision that you may need to make in your life. I will summarise it here so you can also benefit from its simple yet powerful message.

If you have no wealth, money or assets you essentially can only make 3 decisions:

1. Avoid
2. Accept
3. Act

Anything else is just small variations or combinations of these three ways of going about a situation or decision in your life.

When it comes to wealth most people choose the avoidance route. They avoid talking and even thinking about it and hope for the best. They hope for it to go away if they ignore it. Unfortunately in the times that we live in, hope is not a currency I would like to trade in.

Lazy Happy Successful

The second largest number of people will choose to accept their faith and just live with it. They accept that they are poor and that is the way they will live their lives. They usually blame something or someone for their lack of options and just accept their doomed faith. Honestly, in my view, this is still a better option than avoidance. Avoidance creates a constant little voice and pain at the back of your head because you know deep down inside that you can't avoid forever and that the day will come when you will have to pay for your avoidance. You also know that the price you will pay for avoiding the decisions for so long will be far greater than if you had decided in the first place. Acceptance, on the other hand, has a definitive feeling to it. You are at peace with your decisions and can live your life accordingly. You can find yourself some poor friends and do poor people stuff. It is not that bad and because you are at peace with yourself you will probably have a relatively happy life. Avoid blaming things for your situation though, that is the trap that keeps people who accept their reality living an unhappy life.

A small number of people, I am assuming you are one of them, will Act. That means that they will think and understand that the best solution is to act promptly and decisively and live happily with the consequences of that decision. Acting upon a decision is usually the best policy, although we all end up accepting our reality at some level or another. You will just need to find the right balance between action and acceptance for yourself.

Chapter II –

Live Like A Kid

A good friend of mine, Kevin Green, who appeared in the BBC series The Secret Millionaire and who is one of the most engaging and interesting wealth creation speakers on the planet, always reminded me that I must always live my life with the zest for life that a 2 year old has. What a profound statement that is. I can now see that some of the best decisions I have made in my life come from that zestful state of being. They come from the wondrous and pure thoughts that push you into uncommon and exciting spaces. On the other hand, some of the worst decisions come from the opposite side. From the side that is perceived to be the "adult" way of thinking and behaving. These decisions are usually ruled by the fear of loss rather than the pursuit of happiness so even when they are correct they do not lead to your desired outcome.

It is never about the outcomes anyways. Using the perception of our world that a kid uses changes everything. Let me explain this. A kid doesn't look for what is wrong with his or her world. A kid looks for possibilities and happiness in a constant state of amazement. That energy and state of mind are so powerful that if you get to canalise it, your life will forever change and you will never go back to "adulting".

My Phone Call With Douchee

The moment had finally arrived when I got to talk to the guy that was going to turn my life around and take me to a place of happiness and fulfilment. The bonus 10 minute one on one call directly with Douchee had been on my mind for the last 10 days and it was finally here. I was ready, I had done my homework and sent him the questionnaire that mainly asked about where I was financially, physically and emotionally and where I wanted to be over the next 3, 5 and 10 years. It was really hard in my current state of mind to look that far into the future and quite confronting to write down how far I was from that future goal in the present time.

The call was going to take place at exactly 12.10 pm on a Sunday which I found interesting since I would have assumed that a guy with his success record would not be working weekends. I especially wouldn't expect him to be making calls on a Sunday. But here I was waiting and anticipating a turning point in my life and the phone rang at exactly 12.09 pm. On the other side of the phone was the distinctively recognisable American accent of my new mentor.

"How are you doing Dave?" He asked with the same super upbeat sounding voice that he boasted at the event

"I am okay Mr Bragg," I answered sheepishly

"Dave, call me Douchee from now on. And Dave, this is the first problem that I am gonna fix for you today," he interjected, "from now on I only want to hear you say that you are doing great or outstanding regardless of how shit your day has been. Our thoughts and words determine our reality and I need you to be very aware of them. Don't you let yourself down by negative self talk or thoughts"

I had heard this kind of thinking before but to me, it didn't feel right to make up my feelings so I could believe them myself. At this stage with Douchee it seemed too early and uncomfortable for me to raise this point and instead I agreed that I would be doing that from now on.

"That is what I want to hear Dave. This process is about you listening to my experience and amazing strategies so that you can achieve better results in your life. It is going to take a lot of hard work and you are going to be doing a lot of growing up but I can promise you that it will be worth it in the end" Douchee said.

Lazy Happy Successful

Douchee then went on to ask me what my goals were like he hadn't even bothered reading the paperwork I sent about a week before our call.

I still answered happily, "I just want to feel good about myself. I seem to always be doing stuff but getting nowhere fast and I want results. I want to be happy"

"That is what I do Dave," Douchee replied, "I will get you results but they will only come after working harder than you have ever worked before. I have a one on one program that is designed to get you there not in 3 or 5 years but within 9 months. Just like a baby and without the final painful push" he added jokingly

"I am very interested" I tried to reply before he jumped in

"Being interested is not going to get you anywhere, you are either in or out, so what is it?" Douchee asked

I was a bit shell shocked but I knew I needed the best I could get so I said "Yes, I am in." I knew I was 100% in from the moment I signed up at the event so it didn't feel like a hard decision.

"Outstanding answer Dave, my team will get back to you with an invoice and payment options shall the $30,000 investment be an issue for you"

I gulped at the price…. but said nothing

Live Like A Kid

Douchee continued speaking, "This is the best investment you will ever make, you have the world's best wealth coach and I will personally design a program to get you the results you want and deserve in your life"

I felt once again the excitement of starting a new journey, just like I did at the event but was logically terrified of the commitment I had made without really knowing what the hell I was getting myself into.

I then said, "Thanks Douchee! I am excited and ready to put in the hard work necessary, I am a very hard-working man and that has never been an issue in my life." I then got the courage to ask the question that had been floating in my mind during this brief call "Douchee, why are you working on a Sunday? I would assume that you would be doing fun stuff and living the life that I want to live, not calling people like me."

"Dave, that is where you are wrong. For me this is not work, this is who I am and what I want to do to keep being the best. I get to help people achieve more out of life and that gives me more rewards than any time off or material thing ever could. For me, life is work and work is life, there is no difference. When you work doing what you love to do you will never work another day in your life. Weekends are for poor people anyways, wealthy people enjoy life whenever they want to." he ended saying

I felt satisfied with the answer and politely asked what was expected of me next. Douchee said someone from his team would be contacting me soon and they will tell me all I needed to know but until then he said "keep living your best life, or like I like to call it a "Douchee Life", and get ready for the transformation of a lifetime," he then just said goodbye and hanged up.

I had just spent thirty grand to work with a guy that I had only had a 10 minute call with. Was I nuts? Had I been scammed? All kinds of fears and questions popped into my head but deep down I knew I was doing the right thing and that this was the beginning of a fruitful journey.

What If I love what I do for a living?

Isn't that a great problem to have? I get this question a lot and the answer is extremely simple yet rarely do people apply it into action. You should be working on something you feel passionate about and that you enjoy but that work should not be all-consuming. So it is not a matter of what but a matter of how much. You may be asking yourself right now how do I know when it is too much. If it stops you from doing all the other things that make you feel happy and alive then you know you are doing too much of it. So strive to find a job or business that makes you happy but don't let it become your only source of happiness because there is no balance in that and an unbalanced life is a shitty life. You may be telling yourself that this way of living life is not right for you because you know better and you love what you do so much that you will be happy on your deathbed that you dedicated your life to it. Well, once again I call bullshit. You can keep telling yourself that all you want but it will not make it true. You are only doing it because of the indoctrination of achievement you have been subjected to not because you want to do it. In Spain, we have a saying that goes like this "Aunque la mona se vista de sea mona se queda". It translates to: even if you dress up a monkey in silk clothes it is still a fucking monkey. There is no "fucking" in the translation, I just added it for shock purposes and because it felt right. Even if you tell yourself that it is good to be obsessed with work and achievement and that the neglect of your other wants and needs and those around you is justified, you are just kidding yourself, it is a shitty life and that is why you will feel like a miserable bastard even when you achieve great things. So don't dress up your job in silk clothes because it is still just a fucking job.

The obsession with achievement kills your happiness. You are prioritising one item of your life over the rest and that is a recipe for disaster. I see it in every single event I get to speak in. People that have lost their spark because of life's pressures, or so they think. They have dedicated themselves to their job, their partner, and their kids… while they have neglected their inner kid, their happy, inquisitive, adventurous, mischievous, fun-loving kid. I can see it in their eyes, in the way they move, speak and think. They just look and feel old. The good thing about this issue is that it is completely reversible. It doesn't take more than shifting your priorities. The bad thing is that it is contagious. The people that you love the most including your kids and closest friends will see you doing your best version of "adulting" and they will think that it is the right thing to do so they will come up with their best interpretation. People do what you do, not what you tell them to do. You are always leading by example not by empty words.

When I tackle this massive priority shift I usually do it by bringing them back to earlier times in their life. I ask simple yet powerful questions and let them think and speak. Questions like: when you were a kid going into your teenager years what were you passionate about? What about in your teens, what got your hormones going besides sex? Then it is back to pen and paper to rediscover their happy places. I know I have dug deep enough when I see the spark back in their eyes. That is when I know we can create meaningful changes. I like to also ask them: when was the last time anyone showed interest in them and asked them to enumerate and talk about things that made them happy? The answer I get more commonly is, "I don't know if anyone ever did..." How fucking sad.

The death of childhood happiness is not a natural process, it is a learned behaviour imposed by our society. You just have to look at the rest of the animal kingdom to appreciate that we are the only idiots that stop playing when we become adults. If you have a pet or have been around one long enough you know what I mean. As they grow older they don't stop playing and having fun. They are still the same doofus that they were as a puppy or as a kitten. They just add a few adult traits to their ever-happy personality. As the animals with the largest brain mass per weight, we should know better than deviating from what our fellow animals show us: life is made to be joyous in every stage and every moment.

I can hear your whingy and whiney little internal voice saying "but David, I have responsibilities as an adult that I can't ignore". I know you actually just read that last line with your little whingy kid voice... Of course you do, you whiney little bitch! Find a way to fulfil those responsibilities without losing your soul. That is it. It is simple and hard because that means living life by a different set of rules. It means living life to be happy and not to just fit in. It means that the Joneses are the bloody idiots you make fun of not the ones you aspire to be like. And guess what, it is ridiculously hard to make that mental shift because the indoctrination process goes deep. It goes as deep as a colonoscopy. Deep and painful. The pain this indoctrination is causing our society is in my view completely unacceptable as it is the root of most of our current societal problems. We are creating unhappy, battery hen like, sick people. Seriously, think about this. You have your little cage (your home) that sometimes you get let out of to go to that other different cage that you waste precious hours driving to (nesting box) where you work just so that you can make some money (eggs) that are gonna get eaten up by society while you get the scraps. Just enough scraps so you keep being functional. Nothing scares me more than the thought of having to live my life like this. In order to leave the Joneses and your battery chicken lifestyle you need to re-arrange your priorities. Your Ego is going to dampen a lot of your efforts when you attempt to re-prioritise your life and I will cover how to tackle this nasty little havoc maker in our next chapter.

My Grandad Is Still A Kid

I am lucky enough to have had a real-life example of what it means to live like a kid. My grandfather, who is now over 90 years old, is the epitome of this concept. His lust for life is contagious and invigorating. He goes for daily 10km+ walks where he tends to stop and talk to a ridiculous number of people in my small birth town of San Fernando at the tip of Southern Spain. When we go out for a drink in town we can't walk further than 100 meters before someone will shout "Gregorio!!" and here we go again, we stop for another chilled and fun conversation with someone new who will inevitably remind me how cool my grandpa was and still is. He still dances flamenco with his dance group and they perform all over the place. He is always smiling and cracking jokes and regardless of how bad he may be feeling you will struggle to find anything but that cheeky, playful energy and smile. He has a lifestyle plot that he goes to every other day and works very hard on this land to produce veggies and fruits and to keep the place looking immaculate. Some of my most precious childhood memories are in that lifestyle plot and farmlet.

He absolutely loves it there. He had six kids, lived through world wars and civil war, and had to emigrate to Switzerland to find work because the family was otherwise going to starve… Still, you would never guess that he has gone through as much as he has gone through when you first meet him. You don't even need to talk to him, his energy is just different, special, and full of life. He is the kind of guy that people want to be around, the kind of guy that lives the life we all want to live. I am so lucky to have the coolest grandad ever, the best life mentor I could ever wish for.

Kids Teach Us How To Relearn Life

As a father, I have had the privilege of observing this fascinating process first hand. Our kids look at the world in a different way than we do. They are full of curiosity, full of questions, and full of time to have fun and live in the present. They don't worry about the past, they don't stress about the future, they are just there, happy, perfect. Stress, worry, doubt and fear are installed there by society. Kids are free of all those chains and so can you be if you just choose to.

I have talked to several parents who also have had similar experiences while raising their kids. They have remembered what made them happy. They re-learn how a belly laugh is the best way to forget about any problem. They re-learn how mysterious and wonderful the world is when we ask questions about what we don't know. They re-learn that love is not something you receive, it is something that you give.

You see, in my view kids are perfect and then they get indoctrinated into not-so-perfect "adults". Your journey to happiness is essentially a backwards one. You will need to re-learn how to become that perfect kid once again.

In my humble opinion there are three areas that you want to be concentrating your efforts on while on your journey back to childhood:

Curiosity - Joy - Love

Curiosity. Asking questions is the gateway to joy, love and happiness. Being curious lead us to questions that will in turn lead us to relationships, adventures and fun. As we grow older we seem to value people that don't ask questions because they know a lot. Usually, those people are far from happy. They may be professionally or financially successful but I can assure you that real success only comes when you are free and willing to ask questions. One of my favourite philosophers, Socrates, once said: "I know that I know nothing". I know that this paradoxical statement leads to all kinds of interesting journeys but to me one of them is that we all should be content to know nothing because we are always learning, growing and evolving. Having a closed mind is one of the worse diseases anyone will ever have.

Live Like A Kid

Joy. Kids spend a lot of time playing, laughing, and just having fun. We have all heard the claims and studies that say that kids laugh about fifteen to twenty times more than adults. To be honest I struggled to find any really strong scientific study that corroborates that statement but I did find other studies that clearly show that both kids and adults smile more when they do certain activities and those activities tend to be loved by children. For example, Robert Provine at the University of Maryland, which is also my alma mater, found that people are 30 times more likely to laugh when they are interacting with others than when they are alone. Therefore, laughter is a social behaviour, a form of nonverbal communication. Kids learn social and non verbal skills through these exchanges and they thrive on them.

Love. I left the best until last. Kids love unconditionally and without limits. They remind us that there is no better love than the one we give. Growing up tends to leave some scars and we as humans learn to cure those scars by using the love of others. We then start creating a unhealthy pattern in which we seek someone else's love to feel good and fix our problems. This leads to extremely unhealthy relationships and overall unhappiness. Love like a kid and I can assure you that the world will love you.

Chapter III – Redefine Your EGO

Throughout our childhood, adolescence and early adulthood we create and nurture an image of who we are as human beings, our egos. This image helps us make decisions and will determine whether we struggle, cope or thrive in the world. Unfortunately and mainly due to social conditioning, we also attach other things to our EGO. Society and particularly our school system teaches us to attach our job titles, our assets, our partners and even our ideas to our ego. If any of these extra attachments fall apart for whichever reason we feel like we are falling apart. This happens because we feel like a part of us is dying according to our overactive brains. There is no pain worse than the pain caused when you lose a part of yourself, a part of who you are. It causes such a deep and disturbing re-arrangement in our brain that it can make us feel that we just can't cope with the world. The intensity of this internal change causes turmoil in most of our lives and that of the people closest to us. People will do anything possible and then some more to protect their ego and that is when things go wrong. Things go wrong because for example if you attach your house to your ego,

Redefine Your EGO

and for some reason, you are about to loose that house, you will do anything to keep it even if it means screwing up the rest of your life for it. I see this pattern in investors all the time. They attach their investments to their ego and won't sell or change strategy even if it costs them everything. Buddhist wisdom teaches us that being able to let go is the only way you will find true happiness. It also teaches us that attachment is the root of all suffering. When you are trying to protect some of the superfluous rubbish that you have attached as part of your ego, you will do things that will surely lead to more pain and unhappiness. In theory, the answer to this problem is fairly simple: identify which parts of your ego construct are actually worth safeguarding and live happily ever after. In reality, it is a bit harder than that. The introspective process of looking into who you are and being able to pinpoint what is real from what is just a reflection of society and conditioning is a confronting, time-consuming and arduous process.

The rabbit hole into your ego goes deep because when you are truly prepared to enter it, it will take you to the core of who you are, to your real truth. It will lead you to ask those questions that we all seem to be too busy or maybe too scared to ask:

Who am I?

What am I?

Why am I here?

Where do I come from and where am I going?

Is there a purpose to life?

Why do I do that?

What should I do now?

These questions amongst many more are fundamental to your growth as a person. Our busy lifestyle let's most people get away with not dwelling on them because they are "too busy" to think that deeply. Well, screw being too busy, this is the most important aspect of your life so you better make the fucking time to take care of it. No excuses princess.

Douchee's Weekend Event

As part of my coaching programme with Douchee, I was entitled to attend a weekend event where he and his team of experts would teach a group of 100 or so people real-life strategies to achieve more in our lives. It was held at a posh five star hotel right by Hyde Park in central Sydney. As I arrived at the room where the event was being held the music was pumping and very smartly dressed people with huge smiles and ridiculously high energy rushed to high five me, meet me and guide me to the registration table. There I got my manual and name tag and was re-assured that I would have the most transformational two days of my life. The ambient was electric and I was again enthused about the possibilities ahead of me in this journey.

I must say that those two days were indeed some of the most transformational days of my life and my coaching with Douchee. I was completely focused on myself and finding solutions to my problems. The information imparted was pretty damn good and it was delivered smoothly and cohesively in an easy to implement manner. It was abundantly obvious that they had delivered this event hundreds of times because it was a seamless show. We did a lot of work in our WHYs. Essentially, we learned that our WHYs are the reasons why we wanted to change and they determine what that change looked like. We were pushed to go deeper than most of us had ever ventured. Rather than just saying I want financial freedom, or I want to spend more time with my family, we were asked to define financial freedom and how many more hours we wanted with our family and that took most of us by surprise. Most of us had never explored these ideas and we just knew that we wanted more but we didn't know exactly what that meant. We had to enumerate the things that we wanted to have, and describe the happy life we were after; we were asked to specifically quantify the amount of extra time we wanted to spend with our friends and family and we were told to make that time exclusive and special; they made us think and write down a lot and I am grateful that I did so much work during this event because it became the basis of my improved "me". That discovery part of the weekend was the most meaningful introspective work that I had ever entertained. I couldn't believe that I hadn't done this before and that they didn't teach this in schools. Life would have been much easier if I had had these tools and ideas when I was a teenager....

Douchee did all the presenting for the first half of the first day which was emotionally charged and quite confrontational for the participants. There was no safe place in the room and you felt that you had to participate or he was going to hunt you down. Douchee did catch a few of the participants and challenged the crap out of them. He even kicked out one of the attendees because they were not willing to take part in one of the exercises we were asked to do. All this happened in the first two hours of the event! He offered a full refund to the guy who was refusing to do the exercise because he thought the exercise was useless and stupid. Douchee calmly but purposefully explained to him that his time hadn't come just yet and he would be damned if he was going to let one rotten apple spoil the whole bunch. He then asked the audience, "If you all agree with this, say aye"; and an overwhelming "AYE" by the whole audience sealed his fate. The crowd had spoken, he was not welcomed there anymore. He packed up his things, returned his manual and name badge and quickly walked out looking confused and sheepish. Weirdly, that moment made the rest of the audience bond, we had come together to play hard and instigate positive change.

Redefine Your EGO

After that first half of day one, the mood changed. Everyone seemed to be onboard with the process and the techniques. There was a beautifully positive, high energy in the room and at this point, there was a change of presenter. A big Australian speaker took over for most of the remainder of the day and gave us all the nitty gritty of the strategies we would have to follow to get to our WHYs. He was also charismatic and tried to be as funny as Douchee was, but Ben, that was his name, didn't just get there. "Big Ben", as he referred to himself to differentiate himself from another Ben in the team who was vertically challenged, was very interesting and had achieved a lot in his life being one of Sydney's most accomplished property developers and having won several awards to prove it. He covered all sorts of really cool growth and money-making strategies and ideas and I was excited to get going and implement a few of them. What impacted me more about his ideas was when he spoke about relationships, not just about his relationship with his wife and kids but the relationships he formed and nurtured with his business partners and friends. I was lucky enough to have a good one on one conversation with Ben during our lunch break and it was clear he had a skill and a way of "doing life" that I was very attracted to. You could almost feel his high energy and not just because he was physically big and strong but because of the way he showed up and the aura of confidence and fun that surrounded him. To me, it was a big part of the life I was looking to build. I wanted to feel and show up to every occasion like Big Ben did.

Lazy Happy Successful

Ben explained to me that his property development business was not so much a property business but a people's business. While we had our brief one on one during the lunch break, Ben told me "Dave, I was caught in 2008 during the global financial crisis with a massive amount of apartments I just couldn't sell. To make things worse I also went through a divorce at the same time. I was completely wiped out and had a lot of unsecured debt that I couldn't pay at that stage"

I couldn't believe that a man that showed up like Big Ben could have gone though so much financial and emotional strive and still feel the same way about himself.

Ben continued explaining his story "I could have liquidated the business and not paid back any of my unsecured debt but I know who I am and I just couldn't do that. Instead, I sat down with every creditor I had and explained to them that I could not make payments at this moment but that I committed to repaying every single dollar with interest. It took me almost two years to come back from that disaster to break even point. But you know what, two of those creditors are now my biggest project funders and I believe they invest so heavily in me because they now know who I am, what I do and more importantly that they can trust me beyond any shadow of a doubt"

"Fuck!" I exclaimed without even thinking about it.

Redefine Your EGO

"Fuck indeed my friend" Ben agreed. "I do believe that hard times take place to show us what truly matters and what is important. As a result of this tumultuous time I ended up with a much bigger business which is now a publicly listed company; besides that, the relationship breakup led me to a beautiful marriage and amazing kids which makes me feel blessed every single day"

His story wasn't just inspirational, to me it had an incredibly deep meaning. Ben didn't let what happened around him and what he lost change who he was. You see, I have also lost a few big battles but if I was to be honest with myself, those battles took a little something from me that never came back. I let those loses make me less of the man I know I am and after this conversation, but I was now determined to become that confident man that I knew I was. I was going to cure those wounds that had hurt me deeper than I ever admitted to myself and be reborn like a phoenix from those ashes. I had already learned so much at the event but I still felt that the most powerful message of the day was the quick chat I had with Ben during the lunch break.

At the end of day one of the weekend event, Douchee came up to the strategically adorned and perfectly lit stage and made the announcement that we were all "gonna have a few drinks now because if you are not networking, you are not working."

You Don't Own Shit!

"The root of suffering is attachment' Buddha. Ownership is a very western concept that makes our society work the way it currently does. The reality is that you do not own anything, you merely borrow it for a little while. That little while could be a few seconds or a whole lifetime but you can't take stuff with you when you eventually die. Therefore, there are two ideas I want to explore with you further, let me enumerate them first:

The first one is that we attach that stuff to our ego and when we lose it, that stuff acquires the meaning of losing yourself.

The second one is that changing our thoughts from owning stuff to borrowing stuff is extremely beneficial for us.

We are constantly creating and updating the image of who we think we are. Due to our indoctrination into the western, capitalist society, we are taught that having things makes you happier and better. The next step is therefore simple and logical, the more of that stuff you have the better person you become. As a result of that idea, we can also infer that losing stuff makes you a lesser person and that is where the problem resides. Losing stuff becomes a life or death kind of event. The more expensive or meaningful the stuff the more deadly. As humans, we do not think coherently and logically in life or death situations. Our body is designed to move blood from the brain to your muscles and start the fight or flight response which can and will happen even if you are sitting down looking at your dwindling bank account. This response, which was very useful when we were being chased by lions but not so much now that we live largely sedentary lives, is going to create negative outcomes in today's society.

The easiest and laziest way to separate stuff from ego is to have a much clearer idea of who you are and that can only be achieved through a deeply introspective journey. That journey can involve mediation, journaling, deep internal thinking and any other strategy or discipline that helps you understand what makes you who you are. When you go down this rabbit hole make sure you are always aware of stuff you may be attaching to that image of who you are.

The second concept I wanted to explore deeper is that we can easily eliminate most of our life's suffering when we change our thoughts and language which in my opinion is just a materialisation of thoughts and ideas. Thoughts and ideas are like a free flowing stream, we crystallise that stream using words so we can make them easily usable in interactions with other people. If instead of using the word 'owning' we replace it with 'borrowing', it gives it a temporary meaning which completely changes our perception of our reality and ego. A temporary thing is not as meaningful and important as a permanent one, so we will not feel as attached to it. The ultimate de-attachment to temporary things is that most spiritual believes see us as eternal beings, and eternal beings can't be attached to temporary things.

For example if instead of thinking and expressing the thought that "I own this home" you replace it with the crystallised thought "I borrow this home" it completely changes your reality and feelings. Both ideas are essentially right. One of them leads to fear of loss which can lead to frustration and bad decision making, while the second one leads you to feel free and unconstrained and hopefully to make better decisions. This simple change of thought will completely transform your investing. Fear of loss is the biggest hurdle that people have to overcome when I work with them to achieve better results. This is the reason why people lose money in the stock market and why very few people achieve true financial success in the long term. The less attached you are to your money the better decisions you will consistently make, and it is that consistency that will yield results beyond your wildest dreams. When people ask me how I became a multimillionaire before the age of 40 starting with absolutely no money, I tell them that I attribute most of my success to my mindset. At the core of that mindset, there is a believe that I don't care about money. Money is just an outcome of logical decision making and of how much value I add to others. That belief leads me to another belief just as important as the first one: If I lost all my money tomorrow I know that I could easily make it back. These two beliefs will make your investment almost bullet proof. The start to a successful investing journey is an internal journey to your belief system which we will explore further in our Lazy Money Bonus Chapter.

Why You Must Redefine your Ego

Your Ego is just the mental picture you create of who you are. Like any picture or art form, it is open to interpretation. What may look stunning for one person may be boring for the next. Your personal interpretation of your Ego is usually tainted by past experiences, environment, feelings and other people's ideas. That interpretation is so tightly woven that it is almost impossible to separate what truly should be your Ego from what that tainting created alongside it. This is where meditation, breath work and introspective thinking can be absolutely life-changing. Quieting your mind can lead you to ascertain what truly matters whilst eliminating all the white noise that just occupies space and creates shadows that hinder the happiness you are meant to live your life with.

"You should sit in meditation for 20 minutes a day. Unless you're too busy, then you should sit for an hour." Old Zen Proverb. I have very little empathy for people that are so busy that they neglect the core parts of their being. There are so many who neglect their bodies and mind just because they feel we need to do so much mainly to fit into their definition of their Ego. They go into the hamster wheel of life that has a picture of their socially constructed Ego for motivation to keep running. It is no surprise that the majority of people feel like they are not living up to their potential and that there is something they need to change.

Redefining your Ego is therefore an inward journey, it is a journey where you will learn more about yourself and life than you ever thought possible. It is a lifelong journey. It is a journey that if taken without limitation will most likely hugely transform your life, thoughts, relationships and more importantly your happiness.

The other useful tool we have to redefine our ego is critical introspective thinking. Critical thinking seems to be getting harder to find in this busy society obsessed with consumerism and keeping up with the Joneses. A society of sheeple that have lost the ability to think for themselves and rather swallow doctrine and propaganda without resistance or hesitation. Critical thinking is introspective but it can be triggered by listening to or reading other people's thoughts and ideas. Critical thinking lets you assess situations and behaviours from a better perspective. Critical thinking is hard for two main reasons: It takes time and its conclusions can be painful, and as we know people will do anything to avoid pain.

For example, most of us have been in a relationship that we feel is not working. Critical thinking in this example is extremely hard because evaluating a relationship entails a fair bit of effort and depth. You have to go back in time, you have to look at specific moments, you have to look at all the details and the big picture.... it is VERY hard indeed. And all that hard work only to discover that at the other side of critical thinking there will be a resolution, and that resolution will not be easy either. Let's assume that we decide that this relationship is over and we need to put a stop to it. Well, that is never easy because in most situations you will still have feelings for that person and you will also want to avoid conflict. HARD. Or, maybe you decided that the relationship is worth saving because the problems you felt you needed to evaluate are solvable. Well, now you have to work on solving them which usually entails changing your thoughts, behaviours or actions or maybe even changing the thoughts, behaviours and actions of your partner. Conflict = Also HARD. Subconsciously most people know this and that is why they avoid critical thinking to evaluate core aspects of their life. I can assure you that all the happiness you deserve is at the other side of this painful moment, don't even be afraid of it. You will learn about yourself, strengthen your Ego and achieve more happiness than you ever thought possible.

Top 7 Thoughts To Let Go Of To Redefine Your Ego

1. Let go of your limiting beliefs. "A belief is not an idea held by the mind, it is an idea that holds the mind" Elly Roselle. Beliefs based on past experiences are bound to be a part of your ego. Hunt them down and destroy them.

2. Let go of your stuff. You are not what you own. What you own means nothing, it is just temporary stuff that only brings temporary satisfaction. I am not saying that you shouldn't own

anything; what I am saying is that you can't let what you own define who you are because if you lose it you will lose a part of yourself and that never leads to a good time... Your desire for your attachments is what spoils your ego. Having stuff is not bad, loving your stuff to the point that it affects who you are is.

3. Let go of your need to be right. Wayne Dyer famously asked, "Would I rather be right or would I rather be kind?". Admitting to being wrong is hard for people because of the same reason losing stuff is also hard for people. You can associate your ego with the stuff you own or the thought you have. Losing either of them feels like losing a part of who you are. Thoughts and ideas are also just things, don't get attached to them. Have the strength and integrity to always think critically and admit freely that you were wrong or that new data has led you to a different conclusion. It is truly empowering.

4. Your preconceived plan. Having a plan for your life can be debilitating for your ego when the plan does not work out. Instead of a plan you should learn to create potential scenarios and learn to love whatever comes your way.

5. Keeping up with the Joneses. Live your life for yourself not to fit in with society. Always be vigilant of our inherited need to fit in. You will catch yourself going into autopilot to just fit in and when you don't, your ego will scream in agony. Make sure you drown those agonic screams to fit in and strive to be

yourself, to be free. One of Buddhism's four noble truths is that suffering is caused by desire and attachment. I would recommend you read about Buddhism to deeply connect with this concept which can be hard to attain in a society obsessed with materialism, competitiveness and showing off.

6. Your idea of right and wrong, truth and lie. Religion was created as a means to control growing societies. Having similar values means that more people can coexist minimising conflict. The problem starts when you can't adhere to this social construct and you label your action as "bad". This tends to lead to beating yourself up and the beginning of a downward spiral. Religious fundamentalism is the highest expression of this issue and we all know how pernicious it is to society. I have learned to understand that there is no such thing as black or white but just shades of grey. Having this idea of living on a grey scale makes it easier not to label things and you quickly become more objective and empathetic to all situations. This labelling seems to be more of an issue in western society than in eastern culture. Eastern cultures are not so linear, let me explain this foreign concept. In a linear culture, right or wrong are opposites and couldn't be further from each other. Eastern culture is more circular, popularly represented by the round figure of the yin and yang. There are no clear opposites and even polar opposite concepts in western culture are complementary and interconnected in eastern cultures. To me, this makes perfect

sense. Sometimes things that could be labelled as bad, for example being fired from my job at Harrods in 2002, lead to amazingly good outcomes. Getting fired from my job at Harrods was the trigger to my first steps in property investing and self development. So, how can I label an event "bad" when it led to arguably the most financially and creatively positive step in my life? The answer is simple: you can't label it this way, labels are mainly useless. Good or bad only exist in fairy tales and soap operas, and that is why people love them.

7. Your fear of change. Arguably, I left the best till last. The fear of moving past what seems familiar is the biggest tool your ego uses to keep you from reaching all you can achieve. Change is not just external; actually, the biggest change people are afraid to undertake is internal change. It is accepting that you were wrong in your thinking, in your plan, and in your decision. The best way to beat this fear is to think of life and yourself as a fluid being that can easily change course, shape and speed according to whatever it finds on its way. Be like water, just flow.

Chapter IV –
Be The Dumbest Person In Your Tribe

In Spain, we have a popular saying: "Dime con quien andas y te dire quien eres" that essentially translates into "tell me who you hang out with and I will tell you who you fucking are." Once again, there was no "fucking" in the translation but I seem to have created a pattern to emphasise my points whilst translating. If you are lazy or interested in pursuing the lazy way of living you must surround yourself with the right people for your journey. You need the right tribe. Your happiness depends on this simple yet extremely important action. Be ruthless about who you spend time with because as a lazy human, time is our currency and happiness is our favourite product to purchase with it.

Your ego can become your worst enemy when choosing your circle. It is human nature to want to feel validated and loved by others and sometimes this means that we feel we need to be the best in our circle to get that love and validation we desperately seek. Unfortunately, this leads to a plateau rather than a growth phase which is a key component of a successful lazy lifestyle. You will always want to find new ways of achieving more while doing less work and this can only be achieved with the aid of your inner circle. An inner circle that is smarter than you and driven to find solutions and new ways to move forward. What you don't want is a circle that looks up to you for decisions, ideas and work. That is not a circle, that is a failure guarantee. Having a circle expecting that much from a lazy person will surely create an unhappy lifestyle. You will need to continuously step out of your happy place to do things you should not be doing in the first place.

Being lazy requires thought, action and evaluation. Having the luxury to do the things you want to do also means that you will have more free time to think and evaluate. Make sure you do this regularly and are never afraid to take drastic measures. Your objective is not to be liked by others but to love yourself and your own life. Only then you can truly experience the highs that this lifestyle offers which will let you become a reference point for others to achieve similar results in their own life. You can become a real-life beacon of laziness and happiness!

Douchee's Tribe

As we moved into the separate room just about 30 meters away from where the seminar had taken place you could feel that any signs of apprehension or unease that may have existed in the morning were now completely vanished. People seemed genuinely at ease, happy and looking forward to the next phase of the event: the

Be The Dumbest Person In Your Tribe

networking function. Douchee had stated several times during his morning speech that we should be talking to as many of the people attending the event as possible. He told us to ask these three simple yet powerful questions:

8. What is your name?

9. Where are you from

10. How can you help me?

Supposedly the third question was to get us out of our comfort zone and to get into deeper conversations rather than the usual meaningless chit-chat. I quite liked this idea of establishing deeper connections without wasting too much time on pleasantries. I was never one to enjoy chit-chat.

I did think that the two ideas of establishing deeper connections and talking to as many people as possible were not very complimentary though. My thinking was that to get to know someone on a deeper level, you need to spend some quality time with them, otherwise, regardless of the depth of the question, you will never get to see who they are and whether a connection should or could be established. I also thought that by having longer conversations and asking more deep and meaningful questions I would also stand out more from the other people in the crowd that seemed to be trying to emulate the actions of a speed dating meeting rather than a personal development networking event.

Lazy Happy Successful

The room was lit with beautiful chandeliers and a fully stocked bar serviced by two immaculately dressed barmen that stood proudly on the far right hand side from the main entrance doors. Jazz ambience music was playing to soften the environment and plenty of waitresses were also handing out champagne glasses and small canapés. Douchee and Big Ben were already there and they had a queue of people waiting to talk to them. I could easily see that they were moving through the people at blistering speed so I decided to avoid the queue and the meaningless interaction and tried to scope people I felt could be interesting to network with. I did feel a bit judgemental but then I thought to myself that I only had a limited amount of time and my intuition was just another tool I should start trusting and using more. The worst case scenario was that my intuition gets it wrong and I talk to a moron for a few minutes. No big deal, to be honest, I did that most days anyways without any remorse or hesitation. I tried to go much deeper than looks, clothes and other obvious attributes and for the first time in my life, I started looking for energy that I felt comfortable and happy around. I felt that to make the most of my time I should properly meet at least four people that I felt that energy connection with.

The first person that caught my eye didn't look that special at all. He was a short, average looking man with thinning hair and a huge smile. He was dressed smartly in a light blazer, jeans and a white t-shirt. As I approached him to introduce myself he beat me to it and said while extending his arm for a traditional handshake "Hi,

Be The Dumbest Person In Your Tribe

my name is Blake and I am from Auckland, New Zealand. I am just here for the weekend and I ran a multinational online sales business with offices in London and Auckland. How can I help you?" he finished with a smirk.

"Hi Blake" I answered now also smiling and feeling extremely curious about the well-spoken and energetic Kiwi bloke, "I am Dave and I am here trying to find a better way to live my life. What I have been doing so far doesn't seem to give me that feeling of happiness that I crave. I feel that you could help me by telling me more about yourself and your life since I can feel that you exude confidence and you seem really happy. I also wanted to tell you that it was your energy that pushed me to have a chat with you, as I feel that there is something special about you."

"Thanks, Dave" Blake replied. "To me, positively referring to someone's energy is the highest level of compliment that can be given." He quickly continued "I can see that you are not following the rules of the three bullshit questions and you are doing what seems right to you, I like that"

"Yes, I am a rebel" I responded jokingly. "I feel that to make meaningful connections you must give them the time they deserve and a quasi-speed dating questionnaire isn't the answer"

Lazy Happy Successful

"I couldn't agree more" Blake affirmed, "in my business, it is all about true connection and that doesn't just happen with a questionnaire or a script, that happens with empathy and time"

I was extremely curious now to learn more about him and his business so I went on to ask about it straight up "Blake, you have triggered my curiosity, can you tell me a bit more about your business and how you started it?"

"Of course Dave!" Blake exclaimed, "there is no better conversation for a salesman than to talk about himself and his product" we both briefly giggled at the statement. "I was a professional skateboarder until I got injured, after that, my life took a dive and partying and bad choices ruled my every moment. I always knew I was better than that and I got a job working for a large telemarketing team as the first step to regaining control of my life. Within a year I was already their top salesperson and I knew I was ready to move on to the next step of the journey. I got a mentor, actually, his name was David just like you, and I started working for his company as their office and operations manager. The company taught wealth creation strategies and I quickly absorbed all their contents while working for them. I loved it so much that I moved to London and did the same role for a similar company there. After a couple of years, I knew it was time to spread my wings and open my first business. I had noticed I had a rare skillset to sell and I knew there was a gap in the market for a company that could market and

Be The Dumbest Person In Your Tribe

sell through its channels. That is how I created my marketing and sales business. I understood the demand in the market, I was fully aware of my innate ability to sell and all I had to do is to match them in the simplest and most straightforward form possible."

I spent well over 20 minutes talking to Blake and it was the beginning of a great friendship. Not only have we done plenty of business together but we have enjoyed spending a lot of time together doing all kinds of crazy fun activities like driving and shooting tanks in Texas. My intuition was right, reading energy seemed to guide me to a fantastic friend.

After I finished my very enjoyable conversation with Blake I felt invigorated and ready for my next attempt at meeting someone whose energy was right for me. There he was, almost the complete opposite of Blake. He was tall, and lanky and very charismatic. He had that kind of Bill Clinton suave look. He was talking to two people at the same time and his voice resonated as loudly as he seemed confident. Wearing a simple shirt and jeans he looked very Australian if that is even a thing and I was surprised that I didn't recall him seeing at the event earlier in the day. As I approached him he instantly noticed and welcomed me into the group. "Hi, my name is Brad and these are my new friends Justin and Kaz. As I have just told them I am a friend of Douchee and I am his business coach. Actually, I own a very large business coaching company and only do coaching for people I enjoy working with these days. I truly enjoy coming to these events to meet new people and see how I can add value to Douchee's business."

"Wow, that is pretty cool!" I exclaimed while thinking that the follow the energy concept was working out well for me. "If Douchee chose to work with you I am going to get out of my comfort zone and ask you something out of the ordinary" I paused briefly "Can I take you out to lunch tomorrow so that I could tell you about my new business idea and get your thoughts? I know these events are not conducive to deep conversations and I am not keen on just having a pleasant chit-chat"

"Dave, that is a ballsy move" he quickly replied "and, yes is the answer. There is a new Japanese restaurant by the Opera House that I have been wanting to go to. Make a reservation for two and I will meet you there at 12.30 sharp."

The four of us continued talking for a few minutes before Brad politely moved on to another group of attendees and I was feeling excited not just about what was happening now but what was about to happen tomorrow. Brad ended up investing in one of my business ideas and we remain in touch regularly for business and regular social catch-ups. Ballsy moves pay off.

As I turned around about to look for the next attractive energy in the room, a fat guy with a badly fitted suit called Matthew made eye contact and introduced himself. He abruptly told me he could

Be The Dumbest Person In Your Tribe

help me by mentoring me on how to invest more efficiently in the current property market and how to create passive income. His energy was just off, just like his halitosis. I felt repulsed by it and his demeanour and politely yet strongly said "Hi Matthew, I am Dave and I do not need to invest more efficiently at the moment. I do wish you all the best in your endeavours." and just like that, I shook his hand, turned my body away and moved on. It felt great that I was applying something I had innately known for a while but hadn't dared to put into practice. Saying NO is just as powerful as saying yes. I was glad that I got rid of the smelly breath guy and I was certain that from now on that would become my modus operandi.

As I smiled while scanning for my next networking adventure I saw that Douchee went to the front door of the venue where a very well dressed man was standing while talking on his cell phone. As he saw Douchee come towards him he quickly finalised his call and with a beaming smile embraced Douchee in a hug. They both went outside the main hall where everyone else were still networking and having more drinks and canapés. There was something about the immaculately dressed man that just felt different. I could tell that even while he looked like a very busy person, there was a feeling of calmness, and I could even describe it as kindness about him. It was his eyes, his embrace, and his smile that probably gave me the cues that I needed to know. I needed to meet him. I tried to position myself in a spot where I could get a glimpse of them to be able to jump in and meet him as soon as they stopped talking. While I remained strategically positioned to pounce the mysterious guy, Justin and Kaz came over and we had a lovely chat about health and fitness and how our world had lost track of the big picture of what health truly meant. The conversation got so good that I could not be rude and leave when I saw Douchee and the guy with the posh suit embrace once again to say goodbye this time.

I finished my meaningful chat with Kaz and Justin and I ran down the corridor towards the front of the hotel room where "Mr nice suit" was once again on his phone and waiting by the main door next to the concierge desk. A bit out of breath by the time I got close to him I tried to get his attention with a friendly but a bit over the top wave and said "Hi, I am Dave, I saw you speaking to Douchee and I am one of his coaching clients and felt like I had to talk to you for some reason still not known to me. Can I buy you a drink at the bar and have a chat?"

"Mr Nice Suit" extended his hand as I realised I hadn't even tried to extend it myself and as we shook hands he answered "Hi, my name is Michael and I am the event promoter. I have worked with Douchee for years and it is always a pleasure to come down and spend time with him and his clients. I am waiting for my car to be brought out from the valet car park…" as he said that I interrupted "please, let me pay for your car park and take a few minutes of your time while we have a drink."

Be The Dumbest Person In Your Tribe

Michael looked at me for a few seconds slightly confused about the conversation he was just having but still with that energy full of kindness that I detected earlier in the room. Michael then moved towards the concierge and told him "Jono, please wait to bring my car up to the front, I am going to have a drink with a new friend of mine." Jono, a goofy looking South African concierge, quickly acknowledged the request and Michael and I made our way to the elegant hotel bar.

We ended up having a few drinks and talking for a couple of hours about life, business, personal development and most importantly happiness and success. Michael was one of the best networkers in town. He knew anyone worth knowing or was only one call away from knowing them. I ended up attending many of his events that were always not just informative and fun but extremely well organised. His attention to detail and genuine interest to help people achieve more out of life had a massive influence on my life, but that is another story for another day....

After my chat with Michael, I realised that the networking event had concluded and I never even came back to it. I was tired yet elated, and more importantly, I was very proud of myself for having thought of a plan of action and to have executed it with such a successful result. It took balls, energy and determination but it was worth it. I was learning and I was feeling great!

Success And Happiness Live In Your TRIBE

Harvard University started a study in 1938, Harvard study of adult development, which aimed to find out the most important factors that contribute to happiness and success. As we know now, I believe that happiness is success so it is interesting that this Harvard study also put them in the same category. It is an ongoing study and one of the longest ever performed in human history. Do you want to know what the study found to be the biggest factor to achieve happiness and success in your life? Drum roll.... COMMUNITY. Your tribe will determine your happiness.

Waldinger who is the director of this insightful study said that the main lesson you can take home is that "social connections are really good for us and that loneliness kills.". He also added that "It turns out that people who are more socially connected to family, to friends, to the community are happier, they're physically healthier and they live longer than people who are less well connected."

This finding shouldn't come as a surprise to us. Studies of the blue zones, the five areas with the largest percentage of people living over 100 years, also conclude that community is the main factor for their longevity, happiness and success.

What is important to note in these studies is that it is not about how many people you know, but about how many people you know well enough.

Be The Dumbest Person In Your Tribe

Renowned anthropologist Robin Dunbar proposed through his study that humans have a limit of around 150 people they can be close friends with. His findings show that neolithic villages, Roman and ideal company sizes amongst other examples show that 150 could be the magical number. Similar studies contacted by other anthropologists yield tribe numbers between 60-290.

Whatever that number is, if that number even exists, we can be certain that our life and happiness depend on it. Forming strong tribes is the single most meaningful action you can take to achieve more in your life. To me, this concept is so important that I have started a program to assemble and nourish "Happy Tribes" all over the world. Imagine the power of belonging to a group of like-minded people with different skill sets, visions, opportunities, and assets.... All of the units in the tribe helping each other for the greater common good. It would be like networking got on steroids!

People within the tribe would offer help freely or at cost price because they know that a stronger tribe makes them stronger as individuals. The tribe will get discounts, opportunities and deals that you as an individual just wouldn't have access to. For example, if every member of the tribe was to invest $10,000 you would have $1.5 million to invest. Instead of looking at small business or property deals, you could be targeting large ones with more profits and better returns. Not only that, but because of the collective wisdom of the group you would have individuals that could quickly add value to those investments. Your returns would be maximised drastically and you will save massive amounts of time because you will not need to learn and apply new skills that members of your tribe already have.

I can give you another example of how this concept has already worked in our favour through one of my past business ventures. In 2010, I founded a property investing education company that became the largest in New Zealand and one of the largest by revenue in Australasia. We had hundreds of coaching clients every year that were investing big money into the areas that I told them had more potential for growth. Our client base, or tribe, was so large that we were influencing property values in cities across New Zealand! This was great for us as a tribe because we got to enjoy the uptick in property prices which in return let us create more equity very quickly to buy more deals. Our tribe minimise their risk and maximise their returns by investing as a group.

I believe that the reason why we see so many large eastern culture families doing so well financially in western countries is that they use this tribal concept. They all work together and get much better results than they could get as individuals. Not only do they do better financially but emotionally because they know they always have someone to talk to or rely on.

Kill your bullshit-filled ego and join or create a powerful tribe. You will thank me for it.

The Fire Snake

I recently discovered that I am a fire snake according to the Chinese horoscope. Curiosity was triggered and obviously, I started reading more about what fire snakes are like. The part of the description that caught my eye was that fire snakes are masters at delegation and they will look around 30 years old when they are 60 years old because they seek and live a relaxed life. I can honestly say that I have always had an innate ability to delegate and surround myself with people that can and will do the things I find too hard or difficult to do. I LOVE delegating because I love HAPPINESS. I also know that happiness only comes when I give it time. Quality tribes, networking and delegation will make you look younger!

Several studies demonstrate looking at biological markers that people who look older for their age are biologically ageing faster, which will mean that not only will you lose quantity but the quality of life. Essentially these studies show that some people age at different rates. For example, someone that looks fairly old for their age may be ageing 1.2 biological years for every solar year. If this doesn't make you look at your crappy life choices I do not know what will!

Today's culture glorification of being busy and of DIY (Do It Yourself) is only creating old, sick and ultimately unhappy people. Until you unequivocally comprehend and act upon this statement you will not be able to enjoy the abundant fruits of our lazy, happy, successful philosophy.

Online networking is NOT working

Call me old fashioned but to me, the overuse of social media and other online resources is making our networks weaker and our lives unhappier. I honestly believe the world would be a better place without social media. More than social media it is "unsocial bullshit". We should knock it over and spend more face to face time with other humans interacting the way we are supposed to interact. The new generations are losing their ability to humanly connect in face to face social situations. People can tell a lot about others by looking at them and reading cues in their faces and the way they communicate. For example, a recent study published in the Journal of Personality and Social Psychology posits there's a good chance you can tell if someone is rich or poor just by looking at their face. Seriously! You bloody know someone's wealth by just looking at their face!!! This is the reason why it is so important to truly know and meet your team members, and you can only do that face to face. Not only do you need to meet them but you need to get to know who they are and spend as much time as possible with them, obviously within reason. Quality networking is especially essential when looking at wealth creation. I will dive deeply into this topic in future chapters.

I am not saying that social media and online resources do not have a place in successful networking. They do. Their place is the initial "discovery" phase when you are looking for new people to meet and doing some research on who they are and whether you want to spend time meeting them. After that initial discovery phase, you honestly have very little need for online-based communication platforms and most of the communication between you and your network should be done via phone calls and face to face meetings. Avoid texts and emails unless circumstances make them useful.

The Importance Of Fun Friends

Comedy and laughter are essential to your network and tribe. To me, having a group of mates that I can laugh with and truly be myself with is beyond therapeutic, it is essential to my mental and physical health. We laugh, we talk shit, we banter, we argue, we talk about meaningful ideas and we have a crapload of fun doing so. What we don't do is judge anyone or anything, and that is the key and the only way people can leave their guard down and be themselves. Only when you leave that guard down and your true self comes shining out can you have the level of fun that I have with my close group of mates.

Males seem to have an easier time doing so than females. There are several theories and ideas as to why this seems to happen throughout the world regardless of geography or ethnicity. The point that I am trying to make here is that you need this group of people regardless of your gender. I couldn't care less if you think it is hard to find those people. Stop making excuses, find them and hang on to them. Nourish this group with your time and energy and I can assure you that your life will dramatically improve.

People who crave money and power also have a harder time creating a fun network around them. Because they are so concerned about their ego-centred greed they never let their guard down. This leads to them portraying an image and energy that is just not fun to be around. They tend to either be too uptight or overcompensate by becoming an obnoxious clown. Friendships are like a mirror. Fake, ego-driven people also tend to create fake friendships. That is why in my personal experience, a lot of people with an extraordinary amount of money and power also seem to be sad and hard to be around. They have fallen into their ego trap and when you are there, it is incredibly hard to get out. That is why the ego chapter of this book is so important to understand and work on.

Moving On Is Not Hard, It Is Healthy

This idea is going to ruffle a few feathers…. I am amazingly good at moving on from people in my network who don't share my priorities and values. I change, just as other people change too. It is ok to admit and embrace unavoidable change and move on accordingly. Change is inevitable, progress is not. Nostalgia and fear of the unknown are the biggest obstacles to this way of life. You have to identify that those two factors are the ones holding you back

Be The Dumbest Person In Your Tribe

from moving on and then you need to move on regardless of their power. Your network and or tribe includes all your personal and business relationships.

I see so many people postponing the unavoidable by trying to fix broken relationships while wasting precious time that they will never get back. You know deep down when it is time to close that door so that the next one opens. Please, do not feel that I am saying that you need to move on as soon as things get slightly hard or as soon as you hit a road bump. That is not even close to what I am trying to explain. A few bumps on the road are good and healthy for relationships, and they also build strong networks and tribes. These bumps tend to make connections stronger because they lead to real conversations. The key to getting this principle right is to have those real conversations and not avoid them. Only by having those talks can you determine whether it is a bump on the road or a dead end. Have the guts and cultivate the skills to communicate effectively so you can always keep improving the strength of your relationships. I do understand that especially in Anglo-Saxon cultures, having frank conversations or confrontations is not seen as a positive thing. People are terrified of having those confrontations while in Latin culture people seem to understand that they are a necessary part of life, and are less reluctant to go there. I believe that they know that good things do come out of these situations and that is why they have them more often. This is the main reason I believe Latin tribes, networks and families are a lot tighter than Anglo-Saxon ones. Speak up buttercup!

Chapter V –
Lazy Successes Need Better Systems

Lazy people can't afford to waste productive time. As a true advocate of this system to live a happier life you will need to constantly find more efficient ways of getting shit done. It was Frank B. Gilbreth Sr., who was a pioneer in the study of time and motion and an early advocate for scientific management, that first said when it came to hiring someone for a hard job he would always choose a lazy man because "he will find an easy way to do it. He may not do much, but he will find an easy way to do it." A similar quote seems to be attributed erroneously to Bill Gates. Frank B. Gilbreth Sr.'s study of the motions of bricklayers in the 1920s led to the conclusion that the hardest workers were also the most inefficient and that in time this led to fatigue and burnout. Lazy workers were so lazy that they made every move count and it led to less burnout and fatigue.

Clarence E. Bleicher, president of the Chrysler Corporation also agreed with this view "When I have a tough job in the plant and can't find an easy way to do it, I have a lazy man put on it. He'll find an easy way to do it in 10 days. Then we adopt that method."

I have worked with some of the world's best motivational speakers and unfortunately with quite a few charlatans too.... sometimes I cringe at some of their bullshit and quasi-philosophies. Their way of pushing hard work as a way of life to find happiness is preposterous. The average attendee can not consistently cope with that high level of work and performance without burnout. To me, it sounds like an easy pitch to entice hopeful, naive, gullible people. These speakers sell the dream of being a high achiever and that it can be reached via natural skill but mainly through hard work. They then cite a few "hard work" success stories and lead them to believe that hard work will make them happy; and voila, you got a formula to collect a ton load of money duping people. Usually, they talk about famous athletes as a way to sell their hard work and persistence philosophy. They use stars like Lionel Messi or Rafael Nadal who have overcome massive adversity to reach their iconic status. Messi had massive growth issues while Nadal's assiduous and very debilitating injuries should have stopped him from winning tournaments from the very early stages of his career. The reality is that these two "hard work pays off" examples have a tremendous amount of natural ability. They were both gifted child prodigies who also had the resources and an incredibly uncommon mental strength to become who they have become. They started by being one in a billion and then they used hard work to cement it. Unless I sell over

Lazy Successes Need Better Systems

a billion copies I can tell you that you are not that one in a billion, statistics 101, so that philosophy of hard work is just not going to cut it for you. Hard work alone will just get you tired.

Think about some of the best athletes in the world and what they have in common. They make extremely hard skills look easy. Roger Federer's game is so efficient that he has been able to have an amazing career that stretched for two decades with very few injuries. He found a way to be more efficient than his rivals which meant he could produce better performances without suffering as much fatigue and injuries as his peers and making him one of the most successful athletes in history. Even when you look at Roger's physique you can appreciate that he is not muscle bound. He made his skill his main attribute, not hard work or physicality. Messi makes football look easy and the same can be said about some of the best footballers in history. Then, you try to emulate their skills and you end up with a sprained knee. It is anything but easy! Netherlands football superstar, Johan Cruyff, changed football forever with his simple "lazy" philosophy that essentially stated that men could not run as fast as a football could roll. For Johan, it was better to pass the ball efficiently than to run faster. His protege and new maximum exponent of his philosophy, Pep Guardiola, has elevated it to an art form and is arguably one of the best managers ever to coach the beautiful game. This act in itself, elevating someone else's previous work, is beautifully lazy. He didn't rediscover a new philosophy of football, he just copied the one he loved and tweaked it enough to improve it. You don't have to reinvent the wheel, you just need to stand on the shoulders of giants and add your little twist to create your own personal lazy system and strategy.

Douchee's Office Rendezvous

After the successful event and the great networking I achieved, by following a simple plan of action, I became obsessed with planning and systemising. I kept replaying in my head one of the many invaluable sentences that Brad told me over our lunch meeting which will forever change my life: "Working hard is the new stupid". He explained the difference between rich and wealthy by saying that rich people have money but they also have to work crazy hours for it. These are the typical CEOs, lawyers, surgeons, etc… I thought Douchee was in that category and Brad told me he was working with him to get him out of that hamster wheel. He told me that Douchee was a good guy but he had still lots to learn. Wealthy people have money but also have wealth in form of health, relationships and spirituality. Rich was usually ego driven while wealth was a state of mind, a philosophy of life.

As a result of these new thoughts and ideas, time had become my ultimate currency. I started looking at every aspect of my life and worked out ways of minimising time expenditure and achieving more with less. I was determined to be ruthless with any activity that didn't increase my wealth, as defined by Brad, and that took my time

Lazy Successes Need Better Systems

away needlessly. The great interactions I had had with Big Ben and Brad completely transformed my thinking and gave me hope for the future. All of a sudden I felt like I was getting somewhere and that the elusive happiness that I was so desperately searching for was not that far away after all.

While I was systemising my morning routine my phone started ringing. As it rang I thought that this distraction couldn't be a productive one and promised myself that I would turn my phone on silent mode unless I was specifically waiting for a call like in the case of an emergency. It ended up being one of the most important and effective changes that I made as a result of my new life system. Now, I only check my phone 3 times a day and return important calls appropriately. This saves me countless hours of wasted time and saves my mind from having to live in a constant state of reaction and stress.

I did pick up that phone call, it was one of Douchee's team members and he was making an appointment for me to spend some time with him one on one in his office as a part of my mentoring programme. I had been looking forward to spending some proper time with Douchee and the opportunity was finally here so I took the earliest date available to meet him which was literally 47 hours away from that phone call.

The two days that followed that brief call went by in an instant. I was just as equally excited as I was confused. I did not know exactly what to ask or even what I wanted to achieve out of the meeting. I created several draft question sheets but they all seemed pointless when I read them out loud. I was even confused about whether I should ask questions or go more in line with my approach in the networking event and just worry about establishing a meaningful connection which I knew we did not have at this stage.

With all those thoughts floating and creating havoc in my head I showed up at Douchee's offices. I was quickly ushered into a small boardroom that had a large screen tv and an even larger whiteboard. Douchee's books and framed pictures were proudly displayed on the table and walls. I was a few minutes early so I decided to get fully prepared. I had my notepad ready and my phone ready to record every single word that would come out of this meeting. I wanted to listen, learn and connect; I did not want to just sit there being worried about taking notes. My logical thinking and especially my gut told me this seemed like the most productive solution to achieve my goals.

Douchee entered the room exactly one minute before the scheduled meeting time. He was dressed in his signature power suit and tie with a beaming smile and exuding the confidence that had been so apparently obvious on previous occasions.

"Hi Dave" he blurted powerfully while reaching for a handshake, "let's get some amazing progress done today" he affirmed.

Lazy Successes Need Better Systems

Well, that seemed to be it for my idea of chit-chat and connection.... it seemed like today was going to be all about business. I had booked 3 hours with Douchee and I just got a feeling that they could become a very long three hours. I was ready for anything, and I didn't let that negative thought get to me. I felt ready, prepared and in a good mental state to tackle any business talk and create positive actions as a result.

I nodded while shaking his hands and Douchee launched into a barrage of questions. "What was the biggest learning experience for you at the last event?"

I quickly answered "To me, the most important learning experience was that if you are not networking you are not working"

Douchee walked towards the large whiteboard, grabbed a red colour marker and wrote NETWORKING in capital letters on the whiteboard and then asked "How many people did You speak to at the networking event?"

"Four" I responded

Douchee looked at me for a couple of seconds slightly confused and then wrote on the board with a red marker a massive number four with three interrogation signs (4???)

"What has been the biggest change you have implemented in your life over the last few weeks as a result of all the learning you have already done?" he asked

"I would have to say that the biggest change has been to look at several areas of my life and to try to eliminate clutter and systemise my time and actions more efficiently. I still need some help in this area because I…" Douchee interrupted my answer and said, "Not the time for you to ask questions yet Dave, wait until I work my Douchee magic and if you still have any questions afterwards I can assure you that you will get a chance to ask them." Then he wrote again in red and capital letters "SYSTEMS" and he continued by asking "Have your Whys changed since you first started working with me?"

Still, a bit taken aback by his previous interruption I answered sheepishly "Yes, they have changed in that I am more clear about what they are. I still want to be happy, that is the goal, but I now know that I also want to be financially free and have more energy and healthier relationships" Douchee interrupted me again "Dave, that is not your Whys. Those are your Wants and Hows. Your Whys are the reason you go through the hard work that you will need to go through" he explained "So what are your Whys Dave?" As Douchee explained this I realised how far I had gone in my thinking and that Douchee was all about results and reasons rather than the journey. It felt like taking a step back instead of a step forward but I still thought about the questions for a few seconds and answered diligently "I want to be the best version of myself so I can contribute to my family and loved ones and so that I get the time to give back to my community and leave a legacy." As I said this out loud I felt like a fraud. I knew this was just what he wanted to hear rather than where my thoughts were, but I was too afraid to challenge or change the expected answer. "That is much better" Douchee exclaimed while writing down CONTRIBUTION, FAMILY, LEGACY on the whiteboard.

"To me, these things look like real success. Dave, I am without a shadow of a doubt the world's best success and performance coach. I want you to succeed by maximising your performance and I truly believe that this is the path to the happiness you envision" Added Douchee.

To me, it almost felt like he could read my uneasy feeling about the situation and he came up with the perfect sentence to bring me back in line with his program and way of thinking. Within a second of hearing this last sentence, I immediately felt better as I realised that there were different ways to get to the happiness I craved and I owed it to myself and to Douchee to give his way a go. I decided to go all in with Douchee's philosophy and way of looking at results, performance and happiness.

Douchee walked towards me, pulled out the boardroom chair immediately to my right and while he was sitting down he looked me directly in the eye and said "Dave, I need to figure out what is going on before I can suggest a plan of action. Why did you only speak to four people? I know you were paying attention at the event and I know you understood the three key questions and the objective of trying to network with as many people as possible. Why did you intentionally go against the Douchee way?" He asked with a disappointed tone in his voice.

Deep down I knew this could happen and I had an answer to the obvious question but his previous comment disarmed my pre-prepared answer. I did not want to go into why I thought that making a meaningful connection was a better way forward. I now felt that apologising and admitting the mistake of not following the Douchee way was the best answer. "I made a mistake. I thought that it could work better if I only talked to a few key people but I can already see that it was counterproductive to what I am trying to achieve by working with you." I sheepishly answered feeling like it was the right thing to say even if it didn't feel true to the way I felt deep in my soul. I felt that I lacked authenticity but I also knew that fighting at this time could be counterproductive.

"It takes guts to admit when someone is wrong Dave. I respect that in a person. We should celebrate being wrong because that only means that we have found a new and better way forward. This is the reason I have these one on one meetings. They are the only way I can truly break through the bullshit and get to the core of the issues so you can get better results." I gently nodded in agreement.

The rest of the meeting was a full-on smashing of the same strategies, ideas and theories that he had explained at the event. The real difference was that I did not have the chance or opportunity to think or debate. It felt like what people getting indoctrinated into a cult must feel like. It was constant repetition and submission to the ideas of the cult leader. The fact that I had paid such a large amount of money already painted the case that I believed he was right. The way he eloquently added specific real life examples of other students who were in a similar position to me and they achieved some of the goals I wanted to achieve made it completely futile to even contemplate fighting his ideas or plans.

Our meeting ended up with a pledge. I pledged that I would apply his strategies over the next few months diligently and I would write down in a diary my progress and results. Positivity, hard work, affirmations and hustle would be my new way forward. I left feeling tired and a bit deflated, but at the same time still hopeful. It was one of the weirdest sensations I have ever had to this day but I was committed to sticking to the program and finding my long-awaited happiness.

Time Is Your Only Currency

How do you measure whether your system works or not? Simple, if it saves you time it is a good system, if it doesn't or adds up time, it is a dud. You may argue that a good system may lead to cost savings or other enhanced outcomes like better health. I would agree with that point entirely but then I would add that all those improved outcomes lead you to save time which is the ultimate currency of our times and the point I was trying to make.

Ford became the leading car manufacturer by systemising their production process so that they would save valuable time and therefore reduce the cost of production making it more accessible to the masses. Artificial Intelligence (A.I.) will obliterate systems to save us so much time that it will create a society of unemployed, redundant, humans. I am not saying this to scare you but to illustrate that progress always moves in the direction of making production more effective so it saves us our most valuable asset, our time.

We often hear the expression that time is money but to me, it is more accurate to say that time is way more valuable than money. You can always make more money but as of today we can't create any more time, so by definition time is in a different league. Money is just an abstract, made up concept to facilitate transactions; time, in particular the present time, is truly the most valuable asset we have. Maybe that is why we call it "the present", and why it is our most valuable gift.

Lazy Successes Need Better Systems

Every single question and theory that we try to implement in our system should be designed to give us more time. Make sure that you measure that time saving and that you always keep searching for better ways. This is a lifelong journey, not a quick fix.

Question Everything And Then Question It Again

For some bizarre reason questioning anything these days has become a bit of a taboo in our society. Questioning popular narratives earns you labels like conspiracy theorist or selfish asshole. As a science major, I am dumbfounded and terrified about this new paradigm. The scientific method is essentially a way of getting better data and answers by asking more questions. The truth can only be uncovered once we are prepared to ask questions and debate answers openly. New truths will also appear when new data moves into play. This is also true for systems. Systems are only as good as the questions you ask of them. The key to a good system is asking questions and measuring results. Essentially it follows the scientific method of creating a theory and proving such theory through practical applications and data analysis.

Everything in your life is a system, from the way you get up in the morning to your workouts and your work performance. Everything can be systemised and improved and the most successful and happiest people I know do this constantly.

Lazy Happy Successful

It is not easy, but it is worth it. Asking big and little questions will force you to change and most people as we already know are terrified of change. For example, most people that I know who work a traditional job complain that they are tired. That is just a symptom. A symptom that could have been avoided had they asked better questions. In this example, most people with traditional jobs need to use an alarm clock to wake up. Why do you need to do this? I don't see any other animals on the planet that needs an alarm to go hunt or eat some green grass; so why do we need this? The answer is painfully obvious. We are going to bed too late and we are not resting enough, which in turn leaves us feeling tired, cranky and underperforming. You may then argue that there aren't enough hours in the day to do everything you need to do. That argument could become more powerful if we turn it into a question: what things do I need to do so I have enough hours in the day to properly rest and feel full of energy?

Turning disempowering statements into powerful questions will transform your life forever. Try it, it is addictive. I would suggest only making a couple of changes at a time so you can actively measure their results and determine whether they are working or not. If you make too many changes you will find it much harder to find which one you should attribute success or failure to. I know it will take longer this way but in the long run, it will save you time. Trust me, I have been there, and it works.

Lazy Successes Need Better Systems

Your Priorities Are Your Starting Point

One of the things that I love the most about my lazy, happy, successful philosophy is that there is no definite right or wrong. It all depends on you and your priorities. If your priority is to leave a legacy then your systems will adjust so that you manage to do just that. If you prioritise having fun and spending time with your family and friends, you will also adjust your system so that you can do just that. Isn't this awesome? I bloody think it is!

One of the biggest problems I see out there is that people tend to copy other people's systems without having determined their priorities first. This is evidently apparent in popular diets. People copy the paleo diet, vegan diet, lemon cleanse diet or some other diet system that has produced results for an individual or groups of individuals. The problem is that they haven't stopped and asked whether that diet system fits their priorities. This should be your foremost and main question because in my view it is going to determine just how much success you will have with it.

Priorities and values can get mixed up when you go down this avenue of asking questions. I do believe that for the purpose of this exercise they can be interchangeable. Both your priorities and values have to fit the system, otherwise, I can already tell you that it is doomed to fail.

Lazy Happy Successful

Most people are familiar with the purpose of a triage nurse in a healthcare facility. The triage nurse determines the priority of care depending on the initial evaluation results. This is exactly the same thing you need to start doing to better systemise your life. You need to triage your life choices by measuring them against your values and priorities. For example, if your priority is to have a healthy body the lemon diet is absurd and useless. If on the other hand, your priority is to lose weight regardless of health costs then you have the right one.

The triage nurse analogy is the perfect analogy to your life systemisation because both of these processes are ruthless and outcome focused. They both need to ask deep questions about uncomfortable and painful issues. Become the best triage nurse so that you can rescue your life from today.

Chapter VI –
Chilled By Nature Successful By Default

Neediness tends to lead to pain. I was taught a while ago that the key to a successful negotiation is always to need it less than the other person. For example, I have purchased quite a large number of investment properties all over the world in my lifetime. I always go into a negotiation with the mindset that I do not need the property and that there is another deal just around the corner. If it works out I would obviously be happy, but if it doesn't I will not lose any sleep over it. This mindset makes me a much better negotiator than most people in the industry. They are usually driven by either greed or fear. Lazy people have this innate predisposition not to worry about things the way other people do. They are more chilled about decisions and problems. Some could describe them as having a stoic approach to life. A stoic person tends to be someone somewhat unemotional who is not faced or at least greatly affected by adversities or victories. As a professional investor, I have used this "lazy" advantage to make better decisions. For example, it is very easy to get emotional when trading the stock market and having a bad day, week or even a few months of losses.

Lazy Happy Successful

The vast majority of investors will succumb to their emotions and feelings and will end up selling and losing money. A lazy person is more likely to stay the course and end up in a much better position. When it comes to monetary decisions, there is nothing better than thinking lazy.

You should also take the same approach when you get a few wins. Emotional highs can be as damaging as emotional lows and they tend to lead to similar types of problems. Using my previous example about the stock market and my personal experience, I can tell you that I made a ridiculous amount of money by "finding" an obscure stock that went up by just under 600% in the space of three weeks. I let the emotion take over and that temporary sense of invincibility led me to make some of the worst stock purchases I have ever made. To me, this was an incredibly powerful learning lesson and one that I remember in most decisions I make. Emotion, whether high or low, usually leads to painful destinations. Not just when it comes to wealth but in all areas of your life. Those emotional highs and lows are addictive, and like any other addictive substance, you need to be in control before it controls you and your life.

I have found a way of getting my share of these emotional highs and lows in a way that will not cause real problems. I get my highs and lows through sports; both competing and as a spectator. When I play or watch sports, I completely let loose and love feeling those highs and lows. It is a cathartic release that leads me to be more chilled and even tempered in everyday life. My close family members and friends can always tell when I have not had that release of tension for a while and I know that I need it to balance me out. Find your crazy, safe place and let your emotions go wild, then come back to the place where you should be living most of the time.

Was I A Douchee?

I started full of optimism and energy, that was not a problem. Was I committed to following the Douchee way? YES. Was I completely sold on the idea? yes.... maybe.... well... I had doubts. I loved his Douchee method because it was simple to apply and I believed that it had worked for a lot of people, but something at the back of my head kept resisting to go balls deep. Was that affecting my energy and how I applied his principles? Probably, but I was trying with every ounce of my being to hide that small apprehension and show up in a way that would have made Douchee proud.

I was attending every networking event available around me, I was pitching my ideas and trying to get everyone I knew involved in my business plans; I was repeating affirmations constantly and I was working harder than I ever had before. If I was just looking at business results, it was obviously working. I got a couple of great business connections and plenty of investors keen to jump into my new business idea. At the same time, people were weird around me. I noticed that something wasn't right and that they did not act their usual way around me. I wasn't myself either and it all felt wrong, is this what success feels like? I quickly realised it wasn't.

On the second week of Douchee's plan which also involved exercising harder than I had ever done before, I had already injured my shoulder and my knee and could only manage walks on the beach which were refreshing and enjoyable but made me feel like a failure because I wasn't meeting my fitness goals. As I walked along the stunning Manly Beach in Sydney I saw a smiling familiar face carrying an old fashioned longboard, it was Big Ben. He had just finished surfing with his daughter and was on his way back to grab breakfast. Without any regard or hesitation, he gave me a big hug which soaked my t-shirt in cold, salty water. You could see he was invigorated and feeling great so I did not dare make a point about how my t-shirt was now soaked.

"Dave, do you surf," he asked after introducing his super smiley teenage daughter Lily to me.

"I used to, Ben" I answered remembering how long it had been since I jumped on a wave.

"You have to get back into it, mate!" Ben exclaimed, "it is one of the highlights of my day and it sets me up the right way for anything the day brings on. I try to surf most days. I find that I am more effective and happier in life when I surf"

Chilled By Nature Successful By Default

I knew how successful Ben was and that he had a big family while running a big business. How the hell did he find time and energy for surfing? How could he look this energetic and carefree? I was curious and wanted to learn more. "Ben, how do you find time to surf? I feel like I am always rushed and there is always something that needs doing so I never seem to have the time to do this fun stuff"

Ben calmly answered while lovingly glancing at his daughter Lily "Dave, if your life is busy then you must find the time to be present. Change your priorities and life will give you more than you ever thought possible"; then Ben looked directly at me and said "stop fucking around and commit to your best life. I will see you at exactly this time here the day after tomorrow, no excuses" He then hugged me and walked off with his daughter.

I had committed to doing something for myself, something that felt good and something that I thought I didn't have time for. And at this time it hit me. I had started figuring out how to free time up for this activity while just a minute before my brain couldn't even contemplate spending an extra couple of hours on the beach. What had changed? Nothing had changed, the only change was within me. My priorities had shifted and I finally realised one of my biggest life lessons ever: My energy flows where my thoughts go. If I wanted to ever change my life I had to change the quality of my thoughts so that my energy could be directed appropriately. Empowering thoughts create positive energy and solutions; disempowering thoughts create the opposite result. The awareness of this flow would forever change my life and even the lives of those that I love and spend time with. I even caught myself thinking that I wished I had had this epiphany earlier, but then I realised that such a thought was not an empowering one. Wishing that I had done something in the past took my energy away from living in the moment. This was truly remarkable and I found myself smiling like a kid that just got the present he wanted for Christmas.

Not only did my thought process change but my body also started to feel different. A new energy flow opened up and I felt more energetic than I had felt in months. It wasn't the kind of energy spike people experience while having a sugar high, it wasn't the kind of energy drugs provide; It was an energy that grounded me, it made me feel strong, tall and confident. Even my shoulder and my knee started to feel better! Whatever it was I welcomed it with open arms and went on with the rest of my day feeling like I was unstoppable.

The morning when I was supposed to meet Ben for a surf came sooner than I thought. I was there with a new board ready to have fun and not to care about how silly I could potentially look. I hadn't surfed in a very long time and I was never that good at it to start with. But I was determined not to let that detract from the experience. I was determined to have fun and live in the moment without any expectations or hang ups. I got there about half an hour early and just sat on the warm sand appreciating the beautiful surf break. I was so mesmerised by the beauty of the ocean that I did not even see Big Ben approaching me.

With his usual deep, loud voice he exclaimed "Dave! What a day for it! You lucky son of a bitch, you brought the weather and the waves!"

At that stage I realised that the waves were indeed there…. they were fucking huge! My stomach turned and I was genuinely scared about jumping in and making a fool of myself or worse. I think that Ben noticed this change in me and he reassured me, "Mate, I thought about the question you asked me the other day. How do I find the time to do this? I thought that the answer I gave you was too simple. In reality, there is a lot more depth to it. As humans, we are an ever changing melting pot of chemicals. These chemicals are influenced by our thoughts, actions, energy and even the energy around us. When we do things that we love like surfing, we alter those chemicals for hours at a time. Every time I surf my hormonal balance changes, I feel amazing and then I go about the rest of my day with that mindset. I make business decisions from a place of fun and positivity, not from a place of fear. I don't give a shit about how big a wave I ride today, I want to make sure we both have a fucking fabulous time. So, let's move over just a few hundred meters where the waves are tamer. I want you to have fun and to enjoy the moment, simple"

Lazy Happy Successful

To say that I was relieved is the understatement of the century. Knowing that this great dude gave a shit about me and my life made me feel empowered and alive. I was ready to surf and I was more determined than ever to savour every second of it.

I had a blast! I even caught quite a few waves and was amazed at how quickly my body remembered what to do without much effort on my part. I did not feel much pain in my shoulder or knee either. Ben was killing it, catching wave after wave and looking like he was having the time of his life.

As we finished our session we decided to go for a drink at the fresh juice bar in the south end. I was very excited to be able to pick his brains and just learn about him and his way of living life. He was so not Douchee-like… and I was intrigued.

We talked for a good 40 minutes or so and in that time he told me a lot about his business and how proud he was to have achieved what he had achieved but that at this stage of his life he valued other things much more than business success. He said that he changed his priorities after spending some time with a good friend of his. He now was living a more authentic and rewarding life that seemed to flow effortlessly. He even used the analogy of riding a wave which was very fitting to the occasion. I also wanted to be able to just ride my life wave effortlessly and happily and now I could see I was not that far away from it; I just had to find my balance.

Almost at the end of our chat, Ben talked about Douchee's VIP retreat. This year it was going to be held in Bali and the surf there was insane so he was going to make it, and he suggested that I made the effort too. He was certain that the connections I would make in the event would alone make the investment of time and money worthwhile. I had heard about this event but hadn't seriously thought about attending until Ben brought it up. Just hearing that ben would be there I felt that it was the right thing for me to do and I committed to attending, "Ben, I am 100% going to be there then. I will make sure I take some surf coaching classes beforehand so that we can have some epic sessions." I had my new adventure planned now and it felt right. Life was taking the turn for the better that I had hoped for when I took the leap of faith at the event just a few months ago. I was riding my wave.

Energy And Flow

I have learned to listen to and embrace the flow. Sometimes it is hard, some other times it seems to make no sense. For example, as I was writing this morning I felt that my ideas lacked the clarity and flow that I expect and enjoy when I am in front of a screen typing away. I wrote my first book in 2006 and I remember fighting that feeling of lack of clarity and pushing myself to get it finished. I had to fight through the pain and finish like a victorious gladiator in a roman amphitheater. I finished writing that book in less than two weeks but it felt wrong and I was brain dead by the end of it. Things have definitely changed now. As soon as I felt like things were not working, I stopped. I then went to hang out with my dogs, had a couple of pieces of fruit and went to lay down and meditate on my shakti mat. For those of you who are not familiar with shakti mats, they are spiky mattresses that supposedly have a huge range of health benefits. I use it because it feels good and it invigorates me, which is what I needed before I had a 20 minute high intensity interval training (HIIT) session at my home gym. I followed that with a sauna session in my spa room and a cold swim. This factual recollection of events is not here to impress you but to impress upon you the importance of flow and energy. You may be thinking that I went through a lot of motions to get out of my writer funk but the reality is different. I was not expecting to get back to writing more today, I just wanted to do something I enjoyed and that made me feel good. After helping my daughter with her science homework I felt the urge to get back to writing this chapter, the flow was calling me. I did not force it, it happened naturally by doing the things that I love doing.

This book wasn't written in a linear fashion. I went back and forth from chapter one to chapter twelve and everything in between depending on what my focus and energy guided me to work on. I took months off at a time from writing because I wasn't feeling it. The whole process took me two years instead of two weeks, and you know what, I loved it. It feels great and it feels like it was effortless and was meant to be.

When you are in the flow your energy and clarity expand beyond what seems possible. You don't care about the time, food or any other distractions. You are at peace, you are unstoppable, and you are your best self. We can't always be at this level, but when we are it is imperative to maximise its power. We can also try to replicate the actions that lead to this flow and energy spike. To do so you need to first identify the factors that produced your initial energy flow and then you need to start replicating them and measuring the results. The more you become aware of the flow and how it works, the more likely you will be to replicate it at will. Maybe not the perfect flow, but a flow good enough to produce an outstanding performance that will save you time and effort and will lead you to live that happy life that we are all after.

Expectations Versus Affirmations

I bloody hate affirmations. They make me feel fake and cheap. Telling yourself in front of a mirror that you are worth $10,000,000 isn't going to deliver you $10,000,000. Telling yourself that you are fit and healthy isn't going to burn the calories of the 6 doughnuts you ate a few hours ago. The people that I have met who use affirmations regularly are people I tend not to want to hang around for too long. I enjoy and admire authentic character not borrowed hopefulness.

Affirmations epitomise everything that is wrong with the traditional motivational crew. They are all trying to deliver the silver bullet to positive change and they end up delivering a useless bandaid to hopelessly try to stop a large haemorrhage. People use affirmations to trick their brains into believing something that they truly don't embody. I believe that it takes a new level of stupid to try to trick yourself by repeating senseless lies in front of a mirror. It is the "fake it until you make it" solitaire edition.

I have also met people that swear by it and say that it worked for them. These people are the minority and I think that I know why it worked for them while it fails for 99% of the other people. Affirmations can work as a part of a whole. Affirmations, whether spoken out loud or not are the result of internal thoughts and values. People that used affirmations successfully also hardwired a deeper sense of their self image. They first or at least at the same time truly and deeply adopted the idea that they were affirming. They did not expect the affirmation to change them, they used the affirmation to remind them of their change. That is the subtle yet powerful difference. So in reality they never really need the affirmation, they had internally changed through their introspective thoughts.

The real question and the useful exercise would therefore be to rewire your self image so that the affirmations can work to re-affirm your belief system. We should call them re-affirmations then. This is where the TAG strategy that I will describe in more depth in the next chapter is so valuable. TAG stands for Think Act Get. The thinking part is the key and the hardest of the lot. You have to consciously and deeply think about your new creation. Remembering that the creation was always there, you are just uncovering it now. You have to logically eliminate any negative self talk about why this creation doesn't belong there. Don't trick yourself here! If there is something that doesn't add up make sure you either fix it or move on to another creation because obviously, that one didn't work. Once your new creation is solid, you are going to start acting the way that the creation acts. You may at times catch yourself doing things that do not resonate with your creation. Make sure that you correct yourself quickly and stick to who you are. You can always amend your creation but the more you do this the less powerful it will become. Once you think and act like your creation I can assure you that you will get the results. Results follow a system, results are just the final part of the process. This is why success follows happiness and not the other way around.

Let me give you an example of this concept. An out of shape dude wants to get back in shape to enjoy all the health benefits of a slimmer body and to help him get laid. Let's be honest, sex is a massive drive of physical transformations. If he was to follow the traditional affirmation nonsense, he would every single morning spend several minutes looking at his fat belly in the mirror telling himself he is lean and mean and that girls love his dad bod. Well, guess what, he is now just a fatty with a self deception issue and a porn addiction.

Lazy Happy Successful

Using our philosophy, instead of lying to himself, he is going to take the necessary time to figure out who he truly is and why he is in this position now. He will come up with questions, excuses and facts and he will logically dissect them. For example, he will make the excuse that he hasn't had time to train but he knows that is just bullshit. He will also blame an injury he had and he will understand that even if that injury hindered his training and health plan it was not the reason he got fat and let himself go. There will be a moment when he will realise what went wrong and what he believes caused him to let his health and fitness deteriorate. It could be a failed relationship, maybe some issues he had as a kid, the adoption of someone else's system, or maybe it was just a faulty priority system… The reason is irrelevant, the solution is the only thing that matters now. He will now believe in himself because it is true, logical and irrefutable. He will believe that he is a healthy and fit man who deserves to get laid because he does what healthy and fit guys do. He may or may not re-affirm this creation on a daily basis but what he will surely do is to behave and act the way that a healthy and fit man who deserves to get laid (whatever that looks like in his mind) acts. He will catch himself eating pizzas and drinking a bit too much every so often but he will adjust appropriately to fit his creation, and that is ok. The creation in time will yield the expected results and will become his new ego. It is simple math TAG Think Act Get.

Stress And Health

Cancer and heart disease are the two biggest killers in the western world. If we were able to minimise their outcomes we could get people to live longer and happier lives.

According to recent studies, chronic stress on account of reasons like adversity, depression, anxiety, or loneliness can worsen human health. Recent studies have shown that chronic stress can induce tumorigenesis (the creation of new tumours) and promote cancer development.

Studies also conclusively show the direct relationship between heart disease and stress. Stress increases blood pressure and it also increases the rate of plaque accumulation in our arteries whilst making these platelets more "sticky" which leads to clot formation and strokes. Epidemiological data show that chronic stress can be used as a predictor for the appearance of coronary heart disease. Employees who experience work-related stress have an increased risk of developing heart disease. In addition, short-term emotional stress can act as a trigger of cardiac events among individuals with advanced atherosclerosis. Among patients with coronary heart disease (CHD), acute psychological stress has been shown to induce transient myocardial ischemia and long-term stress can increase the risk of recurrent CHD events and mortality.

Lazy Happy Successful

How much more factual data do you need to start making changes in your life? It could add years to your life besides adding quality of life to your years.

The stresses induced by our demanding society are killing us. And this is the key sentence that I want to explore with you. The stress is only induced by your need to fit into society and its inhuman constraints. If you do what everyone else does you will get what everyone else gets. So we need to change, and the only two things we can change are our society or our desperate need to fit in.

Changing society is a process that takes generations. We are seeing the first steps towards a better society with the implementation of work from home and four day weeks practices. Unfortunately, these societal changes are only driven by profits instead of human health and happiness. As part of society, we must share the message that human health and happiness are more important than profits. Only when we truly adopt this view significant progress will be made.

While this change takes place we can implement personal change which is instant and does not require generations to be adopted. Montesquieu said over 300 years ago "If you only wished to be happy, this could be easily accomplished; but we wish to be happier than other people, and this is always difficult, for we believe others to be happier than they are". We have exacerbated this statement by creating social media which makes happiness when

Chilled By Nature Successful By Default

you are comparing it to other people's posts completely unattainable. The simplest way to increase your happiness and health outcomes and decrease your stress is to stop comparing yourself to other people. Figure out what you need and want to be happy and stick to it. Chill out and enjoy life, it is not like you are going to get out alive from it.

Chapter VII – What Are You Good At?

Our school system needs to be looked into and improved desperately. It does not serve our children to achieve and live happy, successful lives. It is basically just an indoctrination process into an unhappy, outdated, sick and inefficient workforce. The core education from early childhood up to university is to create average humans. If you are good at art but bad at math they will ask you to spend more time at math and less at art so you can get a passing grade and move on with your indoctrination process. Yes, from now on I will refer to education as indoctrination because it bloody is just that. Instead of educating teachers to look for each kid's natural talents and abilities we teach them to indoctrinate them into the workforce, into the army of averageness that our society has become. But we can't blame just our educational system for this epic failure. We, as parents, are responsible to make the most out of our kid's talents, skills and passions. The problem is that the indoctrination process leads to an adult prison and you can't help people get out of the indoctrination cycle from jail.

What Are You Good At?

Let me explain how this horrible and inhumane process works. After studying for 15-25 years and usually acquiring a fair bit of debt, the vast majority of adults will have to work 40+ hours just to maintain the quality of life that the marketing we are subjected to deems to be appropriate. They will get paid just enough to get by, usually with the help of personal debt in the form of loans and mortgages. The work you will end up doing will likely bring you to live in a city where you will also be stuck in traffic, commuting to work for hours while breathing polluted air and having no time to dedicate to your health and wellbeing or to spend with your loved ones. Yes, by the time you get back home from work and get through some of your other personal and family chores you will be completely exhausted and mentally broken only to keep repeating it daily. This "lifestyle" essentially means that we are abandoning our children's education and therefore their future and leaving it into the hands of the estate and the media. Spending time with your kids is the best way to guarantee that this inhumane hard work cycle of existence stops. As an adult, the easiest way to escape the cycle is to question everything you thought you needed to be happy. The media has created an image of happiness in your mind and unfortunately, it is not congruent with reality. Question how much work you need to do, how much money you need to earn, what car you need to drive, clothes you need to wear, etc… Keeping up with the Joneses will not make you happy, it will make you poor and a prisoner of the hard work cycle. I should call it the cycle of death because by the time you retire you will be so broken, stressed, exhausted and sick that you will probably not last long before you die. Lazy people understand that there is pleasure, happiness and joy in a simple life. A life that lets you spend the time doing the things that matter, not the things we have been sold to care about. A lazy lifestyle will give you the time to spend with your kids so that they will not fall for this crazy dogma and they will also have a chance to live a fruitful life worth living.

Working on what you are good at will mean that you will not have to work as hard and you will get more time to do other things that are important for your fulfilment. Discover your talents and refine them so that they will let you live a life where you get the things that you want and the time to enjoy them. There is no point in getting all the things that you ever wanted if you don't have the energy, health or vitality to enjoy them.

A Douchee In Bali

Shit! I was excited! I was going to Bali to spend time with Douchee, his crew, plus about one hundred of his VIP clients. I even upgraded to business class to make sure that I got there feeling great and ready to rumble.

The last couple of months had been hard and I needed the break. I was still pushing with every ounce of energy inside me to follow Douchee's plan but it just felt exhausting and unnatural. Yes, business seemed to be going great but it also seemed to be taking more energy and time away from me. I did manage to fit in a weekly surf lesson with a surfing coach but that was about as much fun as I was having. I couldn't help but think that I should have been following Ben's advice rather than Douchee's and that was creating doubt and some form of self sabotage. I felt I wasn't following either Ben's or Douchee's plan and I was caught in the middle trying to figure out what to do.

As I sat on my beautifully appointed business seat and was politely asked whether I wanted some bubbles or juice by a gorgeous air hostess, I could hear the guy sitting in the middle row having a phone conversation. He was loud, I mean obnoxiously loud. Not just his voice but even what he was wearing matched his loudness. He was wearing a pin-striped suit with a green shirt and bright red, pointy crocodile patterned shoes. A massive silver cowboy hat ring on his left hand right just below his huge watch. His look screamed: look at me, I am different. I was intrigued by what he did and who he was so I decided to have a chat with him as soon as he finished his phone call.

Unfortunately, he kept talking until he was told to put his phone away for take off. I patiently waited until the plane got to cruise altitude and we were able to take off our seat belts to approach him. At this stage, he was already working on his laptop and had his over-ear Bosse headphones on, but I was determined to meet him and wasn't going to let his apparent busy demeanour become an excuse not to initiate a conversation.

"Hi, sorry to interrupt your work," I said while I gently tapped him on his upper arm. He took off his headset and looked at me as I continued talking "I love your cowboy ring and was wondering where you got it". I had a feeling that someone wearing something so extravagant would love to talk about it and I was completely right.

"Yeah man, I love it too! I got it in Las Vegas on a work trip about 3 years ago. I love the whole cowboy thing, always have. By the way, my name is Mauro, what about you?" he answered loudly with a huge smile on his face.

"I am Dave, I am heading off to Bali for a business seminar. It is the first overseas trip I have had in a while so I am pretty pumped" I replied

"Nice to meet you, Dave, I am not the biggest fan of Bali but I come here for business regularly. I am a lawyer for a big corporate and we have some great clients here that I need to take care of. I tend to come in, get shit done and fly back home as soon as possible. The tourists and crowds drive me nuts." Mauro explained

I had a feeling he may have been a lawyer, he kind of reminded me of Danny Crane from the hit TV series Boston Legal. At this stage, Mauro's screen saver started up and it was a picture of the Italian national football team lifting a trophy, I was pretty sure it was

What Are You Good At?

the European Cup that they won recently so I asked him while pointing at his laptop "I am a big football fan too, I am now assuming you are Italian, right?"

"Hell yes!" He proudly exclaimed. "football and work are my life. I work over 60 hours per week but I still try to catch all the Juventus games and definitely all my Italia games. The last Euro was one of the happiest moments of my life" Mauro added

"Yeah, Italy played ridiculously good football in the Euros" I added. "I love football too and have always been a Barcelona fan" We then went on a fairly long conversation about football teams and players while we drank a few glasses of champagne, but I was deeply interested to understand his work balance. Sixty plus hours per week seemed crazy and I needed to know how he felt about it. The guy seemed happy and full of life so I wanted to know how he managed to have this much energy after working so many hours.

"Mauro, I got to ask you something. You said earlier that you work over sixty hours per week but you seem to be happy and full of energy, how do you manage that?" I asked

"Well, I am not always full of energy, I can assure you that. I truly love what I do and I feel at peace when I am by myself getting shit done. It is almost therapeutic. I need to be doing something to feel happy. I also know that I am extremely valuable to my company and that it makes a difference to people so that is what keeps me going" he answered. "But I don't think I will keep doing this forever" he continued "I plan to get another one or two more jobs at the CEO level and then either start my own business or just stick to simply working for a few boards of directors"

"Wow, that would be a pretty big change" I quickly interjected

"Yep, but honestly I am not worried about it. I know that I make a difference doing what I do and if the next step never happens I would have lived a very good life" Mauro added

We ended up talking for most of the trip. Mauro was eloquent, ridiculously smart and a very caring human being. We talked, laughed and formed the basis of a great friendship. We have watched plenty of football games together and we help each other in life and business because we have lots of complementary skills and we genuinely enjoy each other's company. I was glad that I paid for the business class upgrade and that I interrupted his work that day. I promised myself to never fly economy again.

The event was being held at an impressive five star resort in the heart of Seminyak. You could see the huge waves breaking from my room's balcony and I couldn't feel happier that I made the effort to attend this event. I was so full of energy that I didn't even unpack before I run down and took one of the expensive looking yet complimentary resort surfboards and went for a fantastic surf session. I felt alive.

What Are You Good At?

Douchee's VIP event was split into several sessions over 3 and a half days. The first one was in the evening and promised to be a welcome and networking get together. I was looking forward to seeing Ben and a few of the people that I had met at past events. As I came down from my room I could see signs indicating where "Douchee's Bali Extravaganza" was going to be held. The signs led me to a nice set up and a cordoned area just by the main bar on the main infinity pool. It was filled with quite a few cocktail tables and a relatively small stage with the backdrop of the stunning Indian Ocean. I was one of the first attendees to arrive and was welcomed with a complimentary cocktail, a wristband, that I was supposed to keep on for the duration of the event and the customary yet irritating name badge. As I walked into the area I saw a guy with 2 cocktails in front of him seating right by the stage. I didn't know why but I got that urge to talk to him that had been so productive and fun in the past, so without any hesitation, I approached the middle age and slightly chubby Asian man. He had a kind, round face and was wearing a Manchester United jersey so once again I thought that it would be easy to start a conversation talking about football.

"So, do you think that United will also suck this year or do you think they can turn it around," I asked cheekily

"No way, we are going to suck even more this year" he answered promptly with a smile. "we have no real good signings and the coach is not creating a team so I am destined for another frustrating season. What team do you support?" He asked

"Barcelona" I answered "and to be honest I think that we are not that far away from you this season although I can finally see some green shoots in the team. By the way, I am Dave, what is your name"

"Nice to meet you Dave, my friends call me Mr Chow, and I have a feeling we are going to become friends" He then asked, "what do you do?"

"I own a small business and do some investing, what about you," I asked Mr Chow

"I am an investor. I have a fairly large property portfolio and I am always looking for new deals and projects. Do you have any real estate?"

"Not yet besides my own home, but I am very keen to expand my investments and buy some" I was interested to get started in real estate investing so he had my undivided attention.

"Well, I am a no-bullshit kind of guy. I only come to these things so I can meet people that will either bring me good deals or will invest in my deals" he opened candidly. "since you have no deals would you be keen to invest with me? I can show you how you can create passive income through property and what is currently

What Are You Good At?

delivering the best return on investment and time" Mr Chow went straight to the point.

"Hell yes. I have been reading a lot about this and I am always open to good opportunities with good people" I answered

"Well, you have a very good guy in front of you. I don't like time wasters and like numbers rather than touchy felly crap" he started explaining " the average returns that my investors make are 7.3% cash flow and 9.4% in capital growth compounded annually. I have been averaging this for 14 years now. What do you think about these numbers?" he finished asking

"Shit, those numbers are good. I didn't think that 7% yields were achievable these days. How much money do I need to get started and what security would I get?" I asked curiously

"A man that talks numbers and asks the right questions is a man I want to do business with" he replied and then answered "I can't be bothered to work with anyone who doesn't have access to at least $250,000. I am worth too much money to waste my time with tire kickers"

His chubby, buddha like face and harmless smile hid a no nonsense sharpshooter. I had access to the money and I liked his style so I answered "that is not a problem, I have the cash and I want to associate with good and reliable people"

"Well, then let's do some fucking business!" He exclaimed while he lifted one of his cocktails for a seal the deal cheer. "I only do business with people who I like Dave, and for me to know that I like you we need to have one too many drinks together so I get to know the real you. Are you ready to have a fun evening Mr Chow style?" He smirked

"Well, I wasn't planning on drinking heavily but you know what, let's make it a memorable one!" I agreed while I wondered whether I had made the right choice….

People kept streaming into the cordoned area. It looked like there were well over 100 attendees, all smiling and seemingly very enthused to be there. The energy in the area was extremely positive. Then, the chilled out music that was being played suddenly stopped and was replaced by Haddaway's hit "Life will never be the same" played at full blast. And as you can guess, Douchee walked up onto the stage dressed completely in white linen singing along while clapping his hands. It was tacky and a bit ridiculous but I still joined in the sing along and clapping just like every single person there did. Douchee's douchebaggery was large but so was his charisma. For the following 20 minutes, Douchee made promises about how amazing the next three days were going to be and how we were lucky to be there with him. He also encouraged us to get to know as many people as possible during the event and to "network like crazy." After he finished his short speech the speakers started

What Are You Good At?

playing "It is my life" by Bon Jovi and Douchee disappeared as quickly and mysteriously as he appeared. Just like that, we were left to network or in my case I was left to drink and party with Mr Chow.

The evening turned into a very late night. the drinks kept coming and Mr Chow was keeping me entertained. His behaviour got wilder and more erratic as he kept consuming copious amounts of alcohol, and so did mine.

I did get to see and say hi to Ben early on in the play. He was surrounded by attendees and seemingly having a blast himself. I asked him whether he was keen on a surf in the morning before the first session and he said he would be out in the ocean by 7 am.

He then introduced me to three of the other attendees whom he had just met and managed to put the basis of a small business deal together with. Ben was a connector and I realised that is one of the reasons I felt drawn to him. He asked questions, listened carefully and figured out paths and avenues for better outcomes. I felt that I was a connector too and I was going to refine that art so that my efforts would be minimised while I maximised output.

The night with Mr Chow yielded one of my most profitable business partners ever. He was unique just as he was also uniquely intuitive at property investing. Did it cost me a huge hangover the day after? YES. Was it worth it? Of course! And you know what, I still made it to the morning surf session at 7 am with Big Ben.

Honestly, the best part of the whole 3 and half day "Douchee VIP Extravaganza" was that first evening. The rest was useful and entertaining but that evening turned into a crazy night and its results were the most memorable section of the trip.

Your Personality Traits

Knowing what you are good at will let you focus your life more efficiently. Understanding your personality traits will not only help in your business life but in your relationships and even your health. For example, if you are a people oriented person you will do better in exercise activities where more people are involved, such as team sports or gym classes. If you are instead task oriented you will be better off exercising with a trainer one on one.

I have undertaken a ridiculously large amount of personality tests. Most of them are pretty interesting but after years of studying and analysing them in detail I have created my very own quadrant to which I have added an extra level twist, creativity.

The quadrant is formed by four personality traits that in my opinion are the most useful ones when trying to determine aptitude and interest.

The 4 traits are then divided into 2 scaled measurements.

The first one is whether you are task or people oriented. Essentially introverted or extroverted.

What Are You Good At?

The second one determines whether you are more emotional or unemotional in your decision making.

These leave us with four main personalities:

- Stars - Emotional and people oriented

- Supporters - Emotional and task oriented

- Bosses - Unemotional and people oriented

- Investors - Unemotional and task oriented

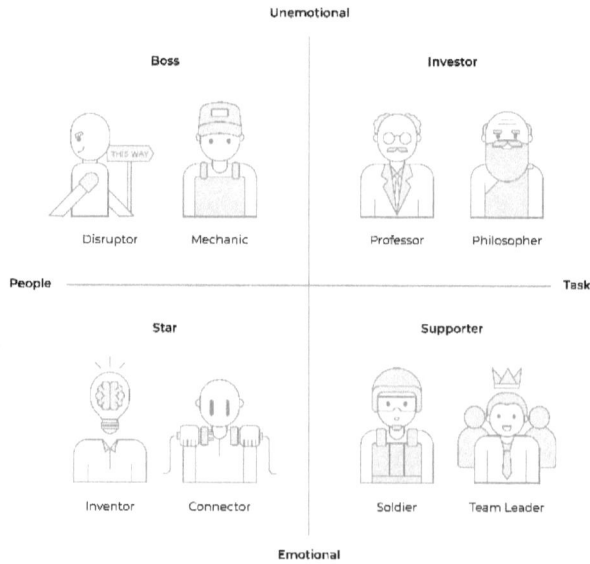

Lazy Happy Successful

I specifically created some of the characters in the Douchee storyline to reflect these personality traits. Douchee for example is a typical Boss. He thrives being around people but doesn't have empathy for them due to his narcissistic traits. He is more creative than logical and that makes him more of a Disruptor than a Mechanic which also accounts for his likability on stage.

Ben is the epitome of a Star. His empathy and the way he maximises his interactions with people make him a clear cut Star. His logic based thinking rather than creativity makes him a Connector rather than an Inventor.

Mauro, the Italian lawyer, is a Supporter. His work ethic (task oriented) plus his emotional nature makes him the stereotypical Supporter. He has the perfect blend between creativity and logic making him neither an Achiever nor a Team Leader but a mix of both.

Mr Chow is an Investor. He is lazy but gets shit done because he is task driven. He loves his own company and only interacts with people when he needs something from them. His creativity score is pretty low making him a Professor rather than a Philosopher.

Now, we need to make a distinction between what you feel you are and what you really are. Let me explain using my perception versus reality. I feel that I don't enjoy being around people. That is my perception although in reality, I am very good around crowds

What Are You Good At?

because I can easily connect with most people and I genuinely care and empathise with their thoughts, perceptions and ideas. This makes me a people person in reality and a conflicted human. I believe that my childhood left me feeling uneasy around people because of my own insecurities. My training and education have led me to overcome most of those insecurities and now I can thrive in those situations. My past still hangs on to the belief that I don't like people but my present tells me that I feel my best when I am around and helping people. It is a self discovery process and one that can lead you to a brand new life full of exciting adventures, authenticity and fulfilment.

Once you determine where you truly belong then you will find it much easier to find something you love doing and that fits your unique skill set and personality. I can assure you that following this simple process will drastically improve your performance. Your work life will never be the same again!

You can also use it for your personal relationships. Understanding what you want in a partner is essential before you even start looking for one. Work out whether you want someone similar to you or someone different that complements you and your life. There is no right or wrong, just whatever feels right for you. The rest is simple, identify and pursue.

In my experience, creativity can be enhanced. Actually, rather than enhanced I believe that the right term to use is restored. I believe that as kids we are all extremely creative individuals and our useless school system corrupts us into not pursuing our creative ways and makes us focus instead on our logical brains. If you want to go into a deep rabbit hole of our pathetic educational system please search the General Educational Board (created in 1903). In a nutshell, it was funded by the Rockefellers to infiltrate their agenda into our educational system. They pumped a truckload of money so that they control what goes into our kids' heads and finally aim to create good workers, not creative thinkers. Not only did they corrupt our educational system but especially our health and food system, but that is a story for another day….

Take on courses that enhance your creativity. Work on your brain and memory like you would work any other muscle at the gym. Learn to play an instrument, learn another language, or do whatever it takes to keep your brain active and connected. Creativity will soon improve and new avenues and opportunities will appear for you.

Setting Achievable Expectations

You do not have to be good at everything and you don't have to do everything. Setting too high an expectation will lead you to failure whether we are talking about business, health or relationships.

For example, I hear a lot of people who run small to medium businesses that they are stressed and overworked because they can't

What Are You Good At?

get any good employees. Most of the time, it is not a recruitment issue but an expectation issue. The business owner is so involved in every major decision and every part of their business that they make it very hard for anyone new to fit in and take over the workload that they were hired to do. Every time that employee makes a mistake the business owner jumps in and takes over or fixes it. The expectation that you are setting for your employee is that you will deal with all major decisions and will take over as soon as things get slightly hard. You are essentially raising spoilt employees; just little children that annoy you more than help you because they know that mummy or daddy will fix their mess. And you know what, it is entirely your fault.

The same pattern happens when we talk about health and relationships. If we set ourselves an unrealistic weight training plan we may soon find ourselves demotivated, injured or just plain exhausted. This pattern leads to failure and eventually, you will drop from the program. The key is to grow within your physical limits and to have clearly defined and achievable goals.

When it comes to relationships one party may overdeliver early in the relationship in terms of affection, loving gestures, etc… once that affection, gestures and/or other not naturally occurring events stop the other party will feel let down and it will at least cause problems in the relationship. The key is to be natural, to be yourself and let the other person love that. If they don't, keep looking.

Lazy Happy Successful

Being achievable is not always bad. Let me tell you a funny story that happened to me at the end of one of my seminars in Australia. I was walking down the road with one of my co-speakers at the event and a good friend of mine to debrief about the event and to have the customary couple of drinks. He is always exceptionally well dressed, with weekly haircuts and beard trims and manicured to perfection. He is also about 6'5 tall and very fit. It is fair to say he is quite a handsome man and he gets lots of attention which makes him even more confident about the way he carries himself. As a good friend should always do, I like to keep him honest and ground his ego every once in a while and I thought I could do so just before we were about to make it to the bar. Two pretty girls were walking towards us in the opposite direction and they made it blatantly obvious that they were taken by my amazing Spanish good looks. As they walked past smiling and maintaining eye contact flirtatiously I couldn't wait to tell my mate he wasn't all that and that I was easily stealing his thunder. His reply was GOLD. He said, "David, you are just achievable. When they saw you they thought they could get you while when they looked at me they thought I was a step too far for them".

I literally couldn't stop laughing, and even if it was just our usual cheeky banter there may be some truth to it. Sometimes the achievable person looks more approachable and will therefore get better opportunities in life. Being perfect or even just being too good is not always an advantage. It is all about the way you think about it and about the way you play your cards. Be yourself, be happy, and be achievable, it ain't that bad.

TAG - Think, Act, Get

This acronym resides right at the centre of the lazy philosophy. Our major advantage as Homo Sapiens is our incredibly sophisticated and almost ridiculously large brain. Every single time that I see a person being unhappy because they are not using their biggest and best tool to find happiness it makes me feel that maybe our brains, or at least a large number of them, maybe going backwards rather than evolving. To me, this is the equivalent of reverting to using stones instead of firearms in a hunt. Yes, sometimes it may yield results but the reality is that it is going to lead you to failure the vast majority of the time. The lack of thinking observed in today's society is due in its majority to two fundamental hurdles:

1. Lack of time

2. Indoctrination

At the risk of being labelled a conspiracy theorist or something worse than that, to me, it seems obvious that the lack of brain usage empowers the elite class while it disempowers the rest of society. If you educate the middle and lower classes into the belief that they need to work hard to be successful and then keep them working even harder by selling them the idea that they need to own stuff to be happy, you have effectively created a very successful recipe for a compliant and malleable workforce. This only leads to one outcome, the rich get richer and more powerful while the poor get poorer and more miserable. The only way to change this outcome is to THINK and jump out of the hamster wheel of unhappiness.

I am a firm believer that there are more than enough resources for everyone to live a great and happy life; I don't agree with or understand the idea of scarcity and that wealth and happiness can only be attained by a select few. If we all get out of this doomed system we will be able to achieve more as an enlightened, thoughtful and happy society.

Do not blindly accept your indoctrination and the constant marketing scams you are being forcefully fed. This is the power of critical thinking and the amazing world that our unmatched brains can and inevitably will create. Once you fully understand the big picture you can start tackling the smaller thoughts.

When you act without thinking you tend to lose. But when you don't act after thinking you are also doomed to fail. This is the all too familiar Analysis Paralysis. Overthinking without any follow through will lead to the same outcome as if you hadn't thought at all. Analysis paralysis can be easily beaten by identifying its root causes which tend to be just basic fears. Fear of failure, fear of rejection, fear of success, fear of the unknown, fear of change.....

What Are You Good At?

The first step to eliminating your fears is to unmask them and bring them to the conscious realm. Fears are big and scary in our subconscious but they tend to be no more than cute little kitties when you think about them consciously. Unmask and think. Once again thinking saves the day!

Once you start thinking and acting appropriately you will inevitably get the results you are after. Start using the TAG principle right away and don't forget to TAG your friends too. The more people you introduce to this simple concept the more success and happiness we will all get as a society.

Male And Female Energy

I believe that fundamentally men and women are more similar than dissimilar but it is blatantly obvious that there are specific traits more widely represented in each of the sexes. By the way, I am not going to enter into a debate about gender identity here. Someone's perception of their biological reality is not relevant to the thoughts I am about to write about. These gender traits are more clearly visible in the extremes of each gender. The ten per cent in the bell curve shows us for example that men are more likely to show physical aggression and engage in substance abuse, and women are more prone to suffer from neuroticism. This does not mean that all women are neurotic and that all men are violent animals.

Lazy Happy Successful

Trait studies also show us that about ten per cent of men have just as many feminine traits as an average woman and the same percentage of women show the same in its reversal. I personally have a heightened sense of empathy, which is predominantly a feminine trait, and that helps me when I speak at events or when I work with people on a one on one level. At the same time, I am very disagreeable which is a masculine trait. This means that I will not bend over to reach an agreement, and will not take no for an answer without a good fight (I am talking about a non violent fight). The reason why I wanted to portray this example is that we all have specific traits that are likely to get us better outcomes if we cultivate them and employ them properly. My empathy would not have served me to lay bricks under the hot sun of southern Spain but it helps me to speak to audiences across the globe and engage them in a way that is fun and productive.

Male energy and female energy do better in specific environments. While female energy tends to deal with people male energy focuses on tasks. This is the reason there are so many more male engineers and so many more female nurses. This concept goes alongside the personality types you learned about in chapter seven. I am all about equal opportunities. The idea that I am trying to convey is that once you understand your energy traits you will find a path of less resistance and that path is more likely to lead you to a happy, successful life.

What Are You Good At?

Scandinavian countries are currently the most egalitarian countries on the planet. As a result, you would expect the gender role gaps to be smaller than those in less egalitarian societies. The reality of this situation is quite the opposite. What studies have found is that the gender role gaps increased as society became more egalitarian. It seems that once equal opportunity was available and the social pressure subsided, people tended to choose jobs and paths that they felt more at ease in. This represents a clear example of what our Lazy Happy Successful philosophy is all about. People with freedom of choice will gravitate to do things that they are good at because they will require less effort and will produce better outcomes. This creates a sense of satisfaction and happiness that permeates through to other areas of your life. Since you are better at performing such activity, you will also waste less time and energy, and that in turn will lead you to a more productive and happiness filled life.

In my opinion, pushing for outcome equality and forcing feminine traits on masculine men will cause massive chaos in our society. We are already seeing some of its consequences in today's society where men are too scared to stand up and speak up. Forcing feminine women to acquire masculine traits will also create the same outcome and it will not be pretty.

Understanding your unique gender traits and using them to your advantage is a massive part of our philosophy. Remember that this is an introspective journey and I encourage you to dig deep and figure out who you are at your core and how it can help you to achieve that life that you deserve.

Chapter VIII-
Know When To Give Up, You Are Not Rocky Balboa!

Giving up has been sold as the arch-nemesis of the enlightened, motivated, positive thinking entrepreneur. In my view and experience, it is exactly the opposite. An early exit will let you explore other options that may be more suitable and successful. Therefore you will eliminate a lot of pain and time wastage, remember that time is your most valuable asset),usually associated with pursuing unattainable goals. Quitting should not be your shameful, big secret. Quitting should be your superpower and should be celebrated!

Stop listening to all the wannabe motivational speakers who are just parroting the same bullshit that has been sold to us for decades, and start being true to yourself and your reality. If it isn't working have the balls to admit it and move on to something that will work for you. What I want to make sure that you do is to develop your own system to help you differentiate between quitting because "things are getting hard", and quitting because "you know it is not going to work".

Douchee Bragg Was Just A DoucheBag

Yes, the journey had been quite an enlightening one but I had had enough of Douchee his quasi-philosophies and senseless regurgitation of cliches. I knew that his philosophy would never make me happy although I was not upset about this seemingly negative conclusion. I felt that this was an essential part of my journey and that I learned as much or even more by witnessing and understanding first hand what I didn't want, than what I could have learned by having been told what I actually wanted. I know that it sounds weird but I felt that Douchee with all his bullshit and douchebaggery had inadvertently helped me more than anyone else could have. He also introduced me directly or indirectly to some of the most amazing people I have ever met. So in all fairness I could only feel grateful for the overall experience.

I couldn't summarise what I had learned during the last few months with Douchee and his team and clients. There were just too many moments of true enlightenment and enriching learning experiences mixed up amongst his douchebaggy pseudoscience. I was now due to have our end of year one on one meeting and I was feeling pretty nervous about the experience. I honestly had very little positives to share about his teachings but the results that I had achieved were undeniably great. I was conflicted because I felt great but did not want to attribute my success to his "Douchee ways". I was feeling happy and angry all at the same time as I envisioned Douchee smirking away when I would tell him that my life was moving forward beautifully. It was infuriating to know that his actual teachings made me miserable and that they mainly served me as a guide for what not to do. But even so, it was undeniable that this process had transformed me into a much happier and more successful human.

Was it his intention to push me so that I would rebel against his teachings and grow as a person? Could it have been a well thought out plan? Surely not… All these questions kept running through my mind while I called his office to confirm the 30 minute appointment for my last one on one with Douchee. The very lovely and overly enthusiastic office lady told me that I was in luck because Douchee had an opening in two days' time. I took it on the spot and for the next hour or so, I kept on ruminating through my questions and the experiences I had gone through since meeting Douchee almost 12 months ago.

The morning of my meeting had come and I went out for a surf beforehand to clear my head and because it just felt right. I didn't need to have a motive anymore to do the things that made me happy. It was one of the parts of the new me that I loved the most. I had been surfing at least twice per week for the last few months and even started getting back into playing tennis which was also one of my passions growing up. The surf was fantastic and I was feeling on top of the world. The night before I had received a short email from Douchee's office saying that the "strictly 30 minutes long" meeting would cover the progress that I had made since I started my coaching programme with Douchee, and it will also delineate the path to take over the next year to keep building on my successes. I had learned enough over the last year working with Douchee to know this meeting was going to be yet again another sales pitch. But please, don't get me wrong, if I attributed my success to the coaching he was providing me with, I would happily sit through the pitch and purchase more. To me, it was all about return on investment now and I was pretty certain that I was not getting that with Douchee, although weirdly, he was the catalyst to my improved life.

I was my usual 5 minutes early and was ushered into a boardroom. This one had twelve large framed pictures of Douchee with celebrities and a huge Douchee logo sign written on the table. More than a boardroom it looked like a cult shrine. I was offered a coffee and water and patiently waited for Douchee while I slowly sipped on my flat white.

Douchee showed up just on time, and as per usual he was boasting a ridiculous amount of energy and good old American style loudness. He barged into the room and came over to me to give me a huge hug. He then said: "Congratulations mate! You did it, you stepped up and your life will never be the same again"

Know When To Give Up, You Are Not Rocky Balboa!

I was slightly taken aback by the over enthusiastic welcome and just quietly mumbled while I was still being bear-hugged "Thanks Douchee, I appreciate it".

Douchee then said "My pleasure Dave, just grab a seat and let's unpack this year and discover new avenues for improvement because I truly believe that this was just the first step of many for you"

I could already see what he was doing. Douchee was as tenacious as he was transparent, so I knew he was preparing the basis for a big sales pitch to keep me in his program. He still had this kind of control over me and I just sat there listening like a good little boy to every word that was coming out of his mouth.

"Well Dave", he continued talking, "you have come a long way but can you tell me what areas of your life have experienced the most improvement? Just pick the top two please"

"I would have to say that those areas are my mental health and my financial position" I answered. "I feel happier than I can ever recall and I have made a couple of business connections that have dramatically spearheaded my financial position"

"That is the power of our network and our systems Dave. Remember when I said that if you are not networking you are not working." Douchee interrupted and then he asked "what do you think your return on investment has been after joining my elite mentoring program?"

Douchee's bullshit on-leading questions were irritating the crap out of me and I felt something inside me snapped. I answered abruptly with a more stern tone in my voice "I can't attribute the returns that I have achieved solely to your program, so trying to quantify the return on investment on your program is an impossible and a pointless exercise"

Douchee looked at me for a few seconds and smiled while saying "Balls!" he kept smiling while he went on exclaiming loudly "finally you got some balls! I love it! This is what I wanted to create when I first met you. You were lacking direction, happiness and balls. Look at you now! You are well on your way to being the person that I knew you had inside all along"

What a patronising and cheeky little fucker Douchee was. I couldn't believe how fast he was at regaining the upper hand and controlling the conversation once again. I took a couple of deep breaths to think about how I would react to his response but whilst doing so I had a beautiful realisation: Through the last year, I had actually learned something extremely valuable. I had to be me, I had to be authentic. I knew I had to do and say what I thought was right without double guessing or hesitation.

Know When To Give Up, You Are Not Rocky Balboa!

I sat up straight, dropped my pen and looked intensely at Douchee. Once I knew I had his attention I replied to his patronising comment, "Douchee, I have followed your teachings and I have spent countless hours convincing myself that the charlatan I could see in you was just a costume that hid a genius who truly wanted to make a difference to people's lives. This shallow conversation has eroded any hint of doubt that I had about you. I can see now that you are nothing more than a used car salesman with some valid, regurgitated content." I could see Douchee's face tensing up and blushing, he literally looked like he was going to explode but I was nowhere near finished and continued my rant "my biggest learning experience during this last 12 months is to do the opposite of whatever you would do. Seriously, your ways make me unhappy, and only through some of the amazing people that I met and my introspective journey have I been able to flourish and feel the way I feel today. I will not sit here and let you take credit for something you did not do. I have had enough of being patronised and sold to. At this stage, I feel that the best outcome for this meeting is if I leave immediately and never see you again."

Douchee did something interesting at this stage, something I was not expecting. He stood up and turned his back to me for a few seconds and then turned back again towards me but now his demeanour had completely changed. He didn't look pissed off anymore, he looked genuinely hurt. He slowly sat down and said, "I have been called a fraud for years, I am used to that. I do all I can to serve others and that includes not only clients like you but my employees, family and friends. I can't be everything for everyone all the time, I know that. I work hard, sometimes too hard. I push myself to be the best version of Douchee that I can be, and yet I still know that this is not enough. I could argue for hours with you or I can just accept that your experience was not a good one and make up for it. I choose the latter. I am truly sorry that you feel this way about my program and I would like to make it up to you." He grabbed a folder that was positioned strategically in front of his seat and took out a single piece of paper. He took out a fancy Montblanc pen and crossed off and wrote something on the paper. He then looked at me and said, "I was going to offer you to renew your mentoring programme for another year which would have required an investment of $28,000 from you. Since you were not happy with the first year of mentorship I would like to offer you a 50% discount for the second year. That means that you would only have to invest $14,000 and because I can feel that there will still be reservations I want to give you something else. I want to give you the opportunity to cancel within three months of signing this agreement for a full refund. If you are not happy with the value you are receiving just let us know and we will give you 100% of your money back. I feel that this will create a win-win situation where you will receive great value without any of the risks and I will get the chance to make sure that my client is happy."

Know When To Give Up, You Are Not Rocky Balboa!

SHIT, he was good. At this stage, I once again couldn't tell if he was being genuine or if he was just a very gifted salesman. Either way, I felt that arguing with Douchee would only create two douchebags. I decided to save time and energy and focus on ending the meeting in a civilised way. "Douchee, I truly appreciate your offer and if it is ok with you I would like to take some time to think about it and come back to you with an answer. I must say that this is the first time that I felt that you were talking with me and not at me, and I am glad that we had this moment."

"Not a problem, I completely understand and will not pressurise you into this decision. I will let our sales team know about our deal so that if you call them within the next week they will know that the ridiculously low price is legitimate." Douchee replied.

"Thanks, this last year has been transformational for me and regardless of my decision about the mentoring, I want you to know that taking the leap of faith to join your program was one of the best decisions I ever made. It pushed me and motivated me beyond my wildest dreams and I found truths about myself that I may have otherwise never discovered. So from the bottom of my heart, thank you." I stood up and went to shake his hand but Douchee stood up himself quicker and effusively hugged me for what felt like a very long time. Finally, it felt like this chapter had come to an end and I felt good about the way it finished.

After the meeting, or should I call it a sales pitch, I was now sure that Douchee didn't have a genius master plan to incentivise growth. Douchee was just another used car salesman pushing his product shamelessly regardless of whether it suited the client. I still wanted to believe in him and his method but it finally dawned upon me that this belief was ill placed with him. It was time to move on and to keep living the way I had learned to live over the last 12 months.

The Square And The Triangle

Have you ever seen a kid playing with one of those plastic toy sets trying to push a square through a triangle? Regardless of how much they push it, the square is not going to get through the triangle, but they keep trying until eventually, they either give up or through a whopper tantrum. Well, in life some things are also not meant to go through and some adults are just acting like little kids thinking they can make a square fit through a triangle. Trying to get things to go through when they are not meant to will just create unproductive work, wasted time and a lot of pain that could have easily been avoided by giving up early in the play.

This principle goes against every motivational coach handbook. They are usually filled with hard to implement real-life strategies and hyperbolised one-of-a-kind stories of superhuman achievement. If you want to live your life measuring speed by the way a rabbit runs when you are a snail, I can already tell you that your life is going to suck balls.

The secret nobody seems to speak about is that you have to understand that you are a square and you will not fit into lots of different shapes. You need to figure out who you are and what makes you happy and strive to get to that, simple. Quit trying to fit into somebody else's mould, you are a unique individual and you fit just fine into your happiness.

Not All Quitting Is The Same

You can quit because you know it is not getting you the outcomes you expected or you can quit because you are not prepared to put in the energy that you knew it would require. One of them is smart lazy and the other one is just stupid lazy. As a lazy individual, you can not afford to be stupid.

The problem between those two is that there is a very thin line that separates them. There is truth to the argument that great rewards usually lay at the end of hard work and hard times. The problem is determining what qualifies as an overcome-able hard time and what is just impossible hard for you. This distinction is even harder to be determined because you are usually emotionally attached to the project (a project can be a business, health program, a love interest or any other you may be involved in). Emotions are usually logics' biggest enemy, and if you can not separate yourself from your emotions and look at the "hard time" with an unbiased mind I recommend that you either get yourself awesome friends who are not afraid to tell you the truth or you get yourself an even more awesome coach.

I see this playing up all the time in the business world. Entrepreneurs invest their time and money into a venture that for whatever reason turns into a much harder ordeal than anticipated. Because they are emotionally and financially attached, these entrepreneurs will keep pushing shit uphill until their legs give up and they just end up face planted on that hill that is now fully covered in shit.

I have a trait that is not pleasant to everyone's taste. I say what I think without much of a filter, especially when it is an area that I am fairly knowledgeable on. This makes for interesting dinner parties for sure.... I am so used to being that critical of myself that it just feels natural to do so with the people I love and care about. Actually, even to the people that I don't give a shit about. There is no ill intent, I honestly just want to save people pain, money and especially time. It is not a trait that I am planning to change, so if you are too sensitive and want to get a sugar coated version of reality rather than the truth maybe you should stay clear from attending one of my events or programs. I can assure you we are not going to be long term friends with that soft-ass attitude. Toughen up buttercup!

Know When To Give Up, You Are Not Rocky Balboa!
There Is No Shame In Quitting

Let me give you some quotes and my take on them:

"Winners never quit and quitters never win" Vince Lombardi - Truth is that every winner has some time or another learned to quit so they could evolve.

"When the going gets tough, the tough get going" Winston Churchill - Obviously this only applied to the Brits and not to the Germans.

"Pain is temporary. Quitting lasts forever." Lance Armstrong - And blood doping only last for a few months...

"If you fall off a horse, you get back up. I am not a quitter." Olivia Wilde - Until you break your back and you need a wheelchair, then you are a paraplegic.

"If you quit once it becomes a habit. Never quit!!!" Michael Jordan - Says the guy who quit basketball for baseball and then quit baseball to go back to basketball.

"Quit while you're ahead. All the best gamblers do." Baltasar Gracian - Or when you are behind and can't come back.

"If you're planning on quitting, first make sure it's not for one of these reasons: Fear, discomfort, anger, self-pity, someone's negative opinions, past failures, unrealistic expectations" Charles F. Glassman - I couldn't agree more, finally some common ground...

"When quitting is done correctly, it isn't giving up – it's making room for something better." Adam Kirk Smith - Thanks Adam, you are speaking my language!!!

I have added all these quotes to show you the power of words and indoctrination. We wear pain as a badge of honour when pain is just the body's way to tell us to adjust our path and choices. We are indoctrinated from a young age to work hard and never quit. We are humiliated, insulted and belittled if we even talk about quitting. Well, this bullshit has got to stop. Smart people quit. Successful people quit. Happy people quit. Quitting is not a sign of shame but a sign of intelligence and courage. Pushing on like a good little soldier is only going to get you killed. I would rather be the general that can call the battle lost and save countless lives than the foot soldier who will jump and run towards no man's land to blow up after stepping on a land mine.

There is no shame in quitting, there is only shame in wasting precious time on a futile activity.

The Retirement Fallacy

There is something you should definitely quit and that is retirement. Working your butt off at the expense of your happiness, fun, family, friends and health just so that you can retire at 65 is a terrible and illogical plan.

Our society got this epically wrong and it has created massive issues that could be easily solved by logical thinking. Before we come up with a plan to tackle this issue let me highlight some of the relevant facts and data available:

1. A study of Shell Oil employees shows that people who retire at age 55 and live to be at least 65 die sooner than people who retire at 65. After age 65, early retirees have a 37% higher risk of death than counterparts that retired at 65. Mortality improved with increasing age at retirement for people from both high and low socioeconomic groups.

2. We have already previously discussed how overworked people have extremely negative mental and physical health outcomes.

3. Elderly people find it hard to get a job because of the perception of low work capacity and the threat of retirement leaving the position open again for the company with the subsequent associated costs.

4. Studies show that a shorter workweek leads to increased happiness, similar performance and much better health outcomes.

The solution is therefore very simple. If we were to drastically shorten work hours and eliminate retirement people would be happier, and healthier and performance would increase. We would also get to use the amazing wisdom that the elderly population have instead of seeing them as a potential problem we could see them as a massive asset to our businesses.

I know that it sounds revolutionary and a maybe even bit crazy but, to be blunt, what is crazy is to keep doing what we are doing to our people. It doesn't bloody work! My plan has the logic and potential to greatly improve our quality and quantity of life as a whole. Imagine being able to spend quality time with your growing family when you still have the energy and strength to do so. Imagine feeling like a valuable member of society and still interacting with people of all ages while adding wisdom and value well into your golden years. Work shouldn't be seen as penitence but as an opportunity to showcase your skills. We can only showcase those skills when we get to work human hours. I define human hours as the number of hours an activity can be done without impacting the person's health or performance. Obviously, these hours depend on the activity performed but you get the point. The traditional 35+ hour weeks are insane and they cost us as a society a crapload of money. The negative health consequences they create for employees and the lack of actual productivity of literally working people to death have to be a tell tale sign that the system is broken and needs a drastic change. Besides that, our ageing population will soon put

Know When To Give Up, You Are Not Rocky Balboa!

so much pressure on pension payments that I doubt you will be able to retire anyways if you are under the age of 50. Time to start coming up with reasonable numbers then, and I believe that the conversation will lead us to work hours somewhere between 20-25 hours.

From personal experience, I can say that working around 20 hours per week makes me happier and more productive and that I attribute this way of living life to most of my successes. Maybe we should all give it a crack, our lives depend on it.

Chapter IX –
The Secret: It Is All About Timing

Growing up in southern Spain meant that the beach was our favourite playground. The Atlantic Ocean around the Gibraltar straight can create some big swells and when going for a swim you always have to be aware of rips. My father fastidiously reminded me that if I ever got caught on a rip I should never fight it. His advice was to go with it, relax, and look to exit it laterally while calling out for help. Swimming against a rip is statistically speaking a death sentence regardless of your swimming ability. This is exactly what I see plenty of people do in their businesses, investments and especially in relationships. They try to swim against the rip; they mistime the moment to enter a relationship; they go too late into an investment or a business venture. The rip, just in case you haven't made the connection yet, represents the timing of the opportunity. Fighting against timing is fruitless and it will only lead you to your doom. To be successful, you need to learn to go with the flow, observe, discern and act only when you are in the right spot to get out of the rip.

The Secret: It Is All About Timing

In the business world, we saw plenty of examples of this in the early stages of the draconian lockdowns that governments ill imposed on their citizens. Businesses and public media used the term "pivot" to define a change of strategy so they could survive lockdowns and their implications. Businesses transformed their sales and delivery systems to fit a new paradigm that they didn't understand and that they had no idea how long it would last for. As a result, quite a lot of the businesses that tried to "pivot" ended up losing a lot of money or going bankrupt. Even the word "pivot" went out of business and was barely used 6 months after it became the "it" thing to do as a business owner. The ones that had some success using this strategy quickly realised that it was just a short term success that sucked up a lot of their time and energy and reverted to their old ways of doing business. Having a major reaction to a temporary problem is the equivalent of swimming against the rip.

Timing is extremely important for relationships too. In my opinion, most close relationships are created because of timing than because of any other factor like physical attraction, mental connection or chemistry. Long lasting relationships start when two people are in a similar life space (aka similar timing) and some other factors push them together. Everyone I speak to about this topic has a similar story. They remember that person they were with or wanted to be with and it just didn't work because it wasn't the right time. So all of you worrying about finding "the one" should be looking for "the one with similar timing" and I can assure you that it will save you a lot of pain and headaches.

Life Without Douchee

After parting ways with my coach for the last 12 months I was relieved and excited to start living my improved life on my own terms; with my new viewpoint and a new hope that was in fact what I was always looking for. The famous writer and speaker, John Maxwell, quote "Where there is no hope in the future, there is no power in the present" made complete sense to me now.

I realised that I loved learning, especially about myself, and that thinking is the most powerful tool in my success and happiness toolbox. I met incredible people that I will cherish and enjoy for a lifetime and who will surely introduce and accompany me to more exciting and eventful adventures. I figured out more about myself and who I was in 12 months than I had done in 30 years. This seemingly little sentence has huge significance to me. Its implications are so vast that it changes your every single action and behaviour. Living an authentic life is my new normal and I am not just hopeful for my future but as a consequence I am powerful beyond belief in my present.

I knew that life had forever changed and that I finally felt stronger and more grounded than I ever did before. I was ready to live in the moment so that I could thrive in the present. My past and

The Secret: It Is All About Timing

future had lost the grip of control they had over me and I was more connected to my inner self than I even thought was possible. The last 12 months were an eye opening experience full of "doucheness" and bullshit but also full of growth and joy. I was now excited for the rest of my life but I wasn't dwelling on the future.

Douchee had his own vibration, his own intense yet contagious energy. I learned to respect other people's energy and vibration but also not to let them affect my own. Getting a better understanding of myself made me naturally gravitate to others with similar energy and that delivered the biggest change in my life. Whether in business, health or relationships knowing who I am, would be the defining factor to succeed. Happiness and the subsequent success were not aleatory, they were inevitable with my new way of doing life.

To me, Douchee was the epitome of everything that is wrong with our current social system and have led to three major crisis:

1. Financial crisis

2. Health crisis

3. Relationship crisis

Douchee had just drank the Kool-Aid and was regurgitating rubbish that may have worked a generation or two ago but it does not work anymore. Douchee was just a cog in the system, a system that enslaves people and stops them from thinking and living on their terms. The system is designed to produce profitable businesses and to create sheep-like citizens. The system doesn't care about your happiness or your success, the system uses you for its own purpose and then spits you out. The only way to escape the system is to understand it and face it on your terms. Once you realise that most of the constraints you have, and actions that you currently do and don't make you happy are there for the benefit of the system, you will never go back to it.

Well, fuck the system. I was free and wide awake and I had never felt happier or more alive. This is my new definition of success: feeling happy, healthy, alive and surrounded by my people. I do hope you find your success and don't meet too many douchebags on the way, but if you do, remember that they are there for a reason and that you will succeed.

Can You Feel It?

I have started several business projects that just didn't feel right. My body and my brain fought me against them even if on paper they looked like good and profitable projects. I can only remember one of those business ventures that I felt off about to finally become fairly successful. All the other ones I felt off about were huge failures. Yes, I am happy to call them failures because they did not produce significant financial returns and to me, that is the primary purpose of a business. You see, timing is not just reading

The Secret: It Is All About Timing

the market conditions, it is also and foremost being able to read the conditions within you. You have to learn to listen to your gut at every step of any project or decision. It doesn't matter whether we talk about a business decision or a personal relationship one. If it doesn't feel right, you should stay away from it.

Besides this, we all go through different phases in our life when we are more likely to succeed with less effort. You have to learn to identify and uncover these phases of your life. This way you will not waste your time and energy that as we now know will only lead to frustration and failure.

For example, I started buying real estate when I was 24 years young. Had I been any younger I truly believe I would have failed to take the steps I took at 24 and I would have failed. This would have led me to make other decisions that would have been affected by the earlier failure and my life would have ended up drastically different. Failures change the way people feel about further decisions and to me, it is clear that we want to avoid failure so our decision making is not obscured and contaminated by our past.

If I had started a few years later, let's say at 28 years old, it would have placed me just a couple of years before the global financial crisis hit. In this instance, it is also probable to assume I would have failed. I can only imagine owning a few properties for a short time before the floor fell underneath you. It would have been terrifying for a newbie investor.

Lazy Happy Successful

I understood at 24 years old that every internal feeling and external event was leading me to jump in without a backup plan. I went in balls deep and put aside any fears or apprehensions that may have led me to make decisions that would have not been beneficial to my flow. I think that intuitively this is when I learned about flow and started following that path ever since with only a few odd exceptions. At that stage, I could not put it into words or truly understand it, but I had subconsciously grasped something that I was willing to unshackle and let free. The decade that followed that decision to allow flow to lead my decisions, was the decade in which I grew the most as a person and defined the path and achievements that came over the years afterwards.

I feel that life is a bit like a forest where we walk mostly aimlessly getting through its steep peaks and flat valleys. Every so often we find a river and what we do when we encounter it determines how far we get. If you are brave enough to jump in and let the current take you effortlessly I can assure you that you will get to places you never thought possible and life will become a much more pleasurable and successful experience.

For anyone that plays sport or has any artistic inclination, understanding this concept of flow is extremely easy because they would have experienced it beforehand. I love playing tennis and some days I get to play in my flow. My movement is fluid and effortless, I foretell what my opponent is about to do before he even thinks about it, and I make shots that I normally would miss badly. In those moments you feel unstoppable. You are the same person that you were earlier in the game but you have found that river and jumped on it and the results are magical. Even writing this book was all about flow for me. I wrote in 4 different major sessions when I felt my flow was just right. Each session was only about a couple of weeks long and I did not force it in any way. It needed to feel right and come out the way it was meant to come out.

Sympathetic Resonance

I do know that some of you may be just a bit put off by my use of the words energy, vibration and flow. I did not write this book for cynical assholes but I feel that it would be good to give some scientific backing. This should quiet that little inner cynical voice that most of us have.

The phenomenon of sympathetic resonance shows how vibration and frequencies can be transferred and shared by similar objects that don't need to be touching each other. The most used example of this phenomenon is a tuning fork. The vibrations of a tuning fork cause vibrations in the air with the same frequency. A second, identical tuning fork that would be hit by the air conducting those vibrations will be made to vibrate with the same frequency that the first fork had. Make sure you do a search and watch a video of this phenomenon online.

You get the same principle with the strings in a well tuned piano, but there is a difference. The strings associated with each key on a piano have a different fundamental frequency. If you play the mid-range keys on a piano with the middle pedal pressed (so that the low-range strings aren't damped), you don't hear the fundamental frequencies of the low strings; you hear their harmonics, which are the same frequencies as the fundamentals of the higher strings. (The harmonics of the higher strings also excite the higher harmonics of the lower strings, but that's a smaller effect.)

We are all just vibrating energy masses. We all have our own frequency. That is why when you spend time close to people with high energy, your energy seems to increase. This is also true when you spend time with people vibrating at lower frequencies and this is why you need to choose carefully how you show up in life and who you spend time with.

Is Timing Cyclical?

Over the years, philosophers, mathematicians and scientists have been intrigued by patterns and what they could mean to us as individuals and collectively to our society. Empires rise and fall following similar patterns and people grow and perish following the same cycle. Nature repeats itself in a precise pattern that we have copied in our buildings and designs. You can easily recognise the phi pattern, also known as the golden ratio, in the Egyptian pyramids, the Greek Acropolis, the Taj Mahal or even at the White

The Secret: It Is All About Timing

House! I encourage you to learn more about Phi and the Fibonacci numbers, it is one of those rabbit holes you will love to get into.

So, if nature, society and individuals are subject to identifiable patterns, our job should be to figure out what those identifiable patterns are and adjust our position to align ourselves with them.

For example, when I exited the Spanish property market in 2006-07 I did so because I felt I did not want to keep owning those properties. It was weird but I remember my wife telling me to sell up because I was a miserable asshole and a pain to be around when I had to deal with them or even just when I thought about them. Then, I started looking at patterns and numbers and it was clear to me that the Spanish property market was not healthy at that moment. The average property price to salary ratio was extremely high, and unemployment was also high and only sustained by the residential construction boom. All while rental vacancy rates remained well above their historical averages. It felt wrong and it also followed a pattern that has led to big drops in value before so the answer was simple: SELL and invest in a better market, a market in a better cycle. On the other hand, NZ as a market felt incredibly good to me and the patterns looked very promising. I went in with it and it was a fantastic ride, making millions of dollars and helping thousands of people along the way to change their lives.

I have had an incredibly positive feeling about the blockchain and what it means for society for quite a while now. The familiar growth patterns are also starting to show up and as you can imagine I am going in for the ride. When both logical and subconscious forces unite and you start seeing signs and proof all around you that it is the right path to follow you have to TAG (Think Act Get) that moment.

Bonus Chapters
Lazy ideas for positive change

This part of the book is here as a tool to induce change. The theory is largely over and I want to focus on practical ways to apply what we have learned.

The way to a lazy, happy, successful life is the way of asking tough questions. I want you to start questioning everything that you do and coming up with better answers for yourself.

As an example, ask these questions as often as you need to and especially do so when you are faced with important decisions or when you need to evaluate things:

Does this make me happy?

Does it feel right?

Does it fit my authentic self?

Is it the right time to do it?

Can I do this more efficiently?

Can I get someone else to do it for me?

Is this creating an acceptable R.O.I. or R.O.T.I. for me (I will explain these acronyms in the Lazy Money chapter)

These are just some of the questions I ask myself every single day. I do this subconsciously these days and it seems that my brain naturally targets the answers that go against my Lazy, Happy, Successful philosophy. My brain creates an uneasy feeling that sometimes I get to understand consciously and logically and some other times I don't grasp in its entirety but still abide by it.

After you get some clarity over these questions I would suggest you start working on your core values. To do this I have chosen a list of values that you should rate from one to ten (one being not important and ten being essential). Take your time to go through this list because it will be a constant resource to come back to when you are faced with life's tough decisions.

Abundance
Accomplishment
Achievement
Authenticity
Adventure / Change
Beauty/Attractiveness
Community
Compassion

Lazy ideas for positive change

Connection

Clarity

Commitment

Communication

Consistency

Courage

Creativity

Economic Security

Education/Knowledge

Emotional Well-being

Environment

Equality

Excellence

Family

Flexibility

Freedom

Fun/Enjoyment

Happiness

Harmony

Health & Fitness

Honesty

Humour

Imagination

Independence

Influence/power

Lazy Happy Successful

Inner Peace

Inspiration

Integrity

Intimacy

Joy

Justice

Leadership

Loyalty

Mastery

Nature

Order

Openness

Partnership/Cooperation

Peacefulness

Personal development

Play

Positive Attitude

Privacy

Recognition

Relationships

Relaxation

Reliability

Religion

Respect

Safety

Lazy ideas for positive change

Self-Care / Self-Protection

Sensuality

Simplicity

Spirituality

Spontaneity

Stability

Success

Trustworthiness

Truth

Wealth

Once you rate all these values from one to ten, list your top 10 in a list and then spend some time looking over them and position them in order of importance to you. The most important value in your top 10 list should be number one.

Now, what I want you to do is compare them to how you are currently living your life. For example, if you spend 60 hours per week working but wealth and success are not even in your top 10, what does it tell you about the changes you may need to make to achieve happiness? Don't concentrate only on the things you are not doing, I also want you to focus on the ways that you are living that reflect those values. Living an authentic life is the only way to happiness and fulfilment.

These exercises are my initial hacks to shake up your system. I believe that the best way to grow from here is to take on a coach or mentor that will help you to keep advancing and finding more about yourself and what makes you tick. Besides a coach or mentor, I also suggest surrounding yourself with a core network of people on the same journey that you are and sharing as much as you can with them. This tribe will keep you motivated and will hold you accountable.

Lazy health

I have always been fascinated by semantics and the power of words in general. The opposite of health is a disease and doesn't that simple word just describe what this lack of health looks like? Dis-Ease. Not at ease. You are at ease when you are not busy when you are just being and enjoying the moment. The other word we use to describe lack of health is an illness. I-LL-Ness. I-Will-Ness. Essentially, when I break down the word illness it means living in the future which in itself is the biggest cause of anxiety and stress. I truly believe that the core of today's health issues has their root in our busy lifestyles and lack of mental clarity.

Sleep can make you healthier and even lose weight!

A team from the University of Chicago wanted to look at how sleep interacts with obesity and so carried out a clinical trial with 80 adults.

Published in the journal Jama Internal Medicine, they found that young, overweight adults who habitually slept fewer than 6.5 hours a night were able to add an extra 1.2 hours of sleep per night after undergoing counselling to improve their sleeping habits. Over three years, this led to an average weight loss of 12 kgs – simply by sleeping more!

The results showed that getting more sleep reduced people's overall caloric intake by an average of 270 calories per day, with some people consuming a whooping 500 fewer calories.

Dr Esra Tasali, from the University of Chicago's sleep centre, said the study had not intended to look at weight loss.

"But even within just two weeks, we have quantified evidence showing a decrease in caloric intake and a negative energy balance – caloric intake is less than calories burned," she said.

"If healthy sleep habits are maintained over a longer duration this would lead to clinically important weight loss over time. Many people are working hard to find ways to decrease their caloric intake to lose weight – well, just by sleeping more, you may be able to reduce it substantially."

You see, as I keep repeating, sometimes doing less achieves more. So make sure you get your beauty sleep, princess!

Managing your weight. The obesity epidemic problem

Managing your weight in a sustainable and lasting manner is a simple two step formula.

Lazy health

First, eat appropriately to lower your body weight to a reasonable level. I am personally a huge fan of intermittent fasting. I follow a 17-7 cycle which means that I can eat from 12 pm until 7 pm and fast for the other 17 hours. I find it extremely easy to follow and it keeps my weight down so that I minimise injuries in my training program and everyday life activities. I recommend that you have a look at all the fasting diets out there and give a few a go to find out which one fits you better. The benefits are truly amazing.

Secondly, add an appropriate exercise routine to step up your health gains. To me, people undertaking strenuous workouts while carrying a lot of extra weight seems like a ticking time bomb. Your joints can barely cope with your weight and you are increasing pressure and impact on them on a ridiculous basis. Injuries will happen and they will slow your progress if not completely halt it. Watching tv programs like The Biggest Loser makes me cringe and shows me all that is wrong with society. The search for the magical silver bullet through incredibly hard, inhumane and dangerous work. As I keep reminding you throughout this book, less is more. Adapt your body slowly so you minimise risks and maximise results. I know it is not sexy to say this but it bloody works!

This is where I need to remind you that you don't have to look like a model unless you are one. To me, that level of physical stress can only lead to bad outcomes. This is why I hate social media and those "assholy" influencers showing off their sculpted bodies and telling you that you are not good enough unless you look like them. Well, fuck you! Every single one of those wannabes I have ever met (and I have met a lot of them) are miserable losers with so many issues that they can barely manage to make it through the day without breaking down in tears every hour or so. Being healthy and happy beats physical obsession every single day. Remember this while you scroll through the bullshit social media feed on your device. Do one better: stop scrolling and start living!

My favourite Lazy health trick

Use a sauna. That is it. Use it as much as you can because the results will astound you. Here is a list of some of the benefits you will experience while you just sit down, relax and enjoy:

1. Cardiovascular health improvement. Using the sauna regularly has been proven to decrease the risk of cardiovascular disease by at least 65%

2. Better skin. Due to better skin oxygenation through enhanced capillary circulation.

3. Improved immune system. Reduce your risk of catching a cold or flu by over 30%.

4. Pain relief and increased mobility. Due to its anti-inflammatory properties using the sauna will help you to reduce pain and move more freely.

5. Hormone regulation improvement. Improve growth hormone production and insulin sensitivity. This means that you will increase and keep more muscle mass.

6. Better sleep. The use of a sauna produces a deeper relaxation that leads to deeper and more restorative sleeping patterns.

7. Improve muscle recovery. The improved circulation eliminates waste products and delivers healthy energy to your muscles.

8. Improve your stress responses. Putting your body under controlled stress leads to developing resilience. If you want to take this resilience training to the next level mix ice baths or cold showers with your sauna.

I use my sauna at least 5 times per week and to me, it has been a game changer.

Here is some data from actual studies on the use of saunas (Laukkanen et al 2018; Patrick 2021; Zaccardi et al 2017):

65% reduced risk of Alzheimer's

63% reduced heart disease mortality

50% lower fatal cardiovascular disease

48% lower fatal coronary heart disease

47% reduced risk of pneumonia

46% lower risk of hypertension

41% fewer respiratory diseases

Fewer symptoms of depression

Common colds cut in half

40% reduced risk of all cause mortality!!!

If you are struggling to start exercising I would recommend that you instead start using a sauna for a month or two to improve your cardiovascular system and get your body ready to face the stress that exercise provides. This is the perfect first step for the lazy ones and for people who have never exercised properly before.

Another great tip is to use BFR or KAATSU bands. Blood Flow Restriction (BFR) is used to produce high intensity results using lower resistance. It has been traditionally used mainly for the elderly or for people recovering from injuries. I personally use it to target my weakest muscles and to get outstanding results with minimum effort and risk. There is a plethora of information available online for you to dive right into it so you can incorporate it into your routines. Don't work out harder, work smarter and feel better.

Maximise your hormonal cycle

Men and women differ in the way their hormonal cycles work. While women are more affected by their monthly cycle men are more affected by their testosterone production daily cycle. According to research from the University of Louisville, Testosterone levels peak first thing in the morning to abruptly drop until late morning to early afternoon when they tend to spike again. Once that spike takes place the testosterone level will decrease to be at its lowest through in the evening hours. Every man presents slightly different variations but my point here is that you need to understand your biorhythm to make better decisions. For example, you should never hit the gym when your testosterone is at its lowest, just like you probably shouldn't attend negotiations whilst your testosterone level is at its peak. Understanding your body and allocating activities to adequate hours will save you a lot of money, time and headaches. This is the micro cycle of testosterone production but you should also understand that there is an annual and a lifetime macrocycle. Testosterone production diminishes as we age once we reach peak production which usually happens in our 20s. The 20s and 30s are the years when men tend to make bold decisions and it correlates nicely with their testosterone production. These years are full of ups and downs but men don't tend to be as productive as they become in their 40s, 50s and 60s. Testosterone production may have to do a lot with this fact. Men see the world differently once their testosterone level drops to a slightly lower level.

On an annual basis, testosterone production tends to have a peak in the summer months, October in the northern hemisphere, and April (regardless of the hemisphere where you live) which is a very interesting pattern. Another interesting correlation is that financial crisis historically take place in the last quarter of the year (September onwards). If you are going to make large investments or purchases it may pay off to do those in April while if you are going to undertake an intense project, like a new business or a new exercise program to gain muscle, you may be better off to do so in August if you are in the northern hemisphere to take advantage of the summer and October peaks.

There is plenty of literature dedicated to female monthly cycles but the point I am making still applies. Choose to do activities that correlate to your hormonal cycle so you are not pushing shit uphill and fighting battles in every corner.

Female cycles are often broken down into 4 stages:

The Menstrual Cycle.

Usually between 3 and 7 days long. This is a period of weakness. Rather than doing strenuous activities, you should focus on relaxing activities to promote recovery and well being. Yoga, meditation, breathing exercises, reading, walks, etc… Spain is the first country to have introduced legislation for females to be able to take time off during this part of their cycle. To me, this seems like a fantastic move that will increase productivity, health, and especially well being.

The Follicular Phase.

Your body starts producing FSH so eggs can be produced. Oestrogen also peaks to build up the uterine lining but at the same time, this hormone peak will boost your energy, mood and libido. This is the part of your monthly cycle where you should socialise and tackle bigger projects.

The Ovulation Phase

Luteinizing hormone is released so your ovaries release eggs. Progesterone is also released in this phase. You will feel more balanced and strong during this phase and you will feel like you can accomplish more and deal with problems more easily. Use this to your advantage in every aspect of your life.

The luteal Phase.

This phase occurs right after ovulation ends. You can divide it into two halves. In the first half, you will still feel really good but a big drop in androgens and or imbalances in your oestrogen will trigger massive changes to your mood and overall feeling. This is the infamous PMS, and we all know how bad it can get. Eliminate meetings and negotiations from this phase and focus on your mindfulness, health and diet.

Our society has created work and play patterns that are just plain stupid when compared to our hormonal cycles. Society could be happier and more productive if we just listened to our bodies rather than the mindless greed and the sadistic philosophy of working through any level of pain to achieve more. Working hard is the new stupid.

Stop eating SHIT

Seriously, this has gone out of control in our society and it is causing a tremendous amount of pain and suffering.

The first issue we need to address is that we eat too much. We don't need nearly as much quantity of food as what we are forcing down our throats. The real issue is that our bodies are starving even after we put that much food down our gobble because the food we are consuming is nutrient deficient. There are two main reasons our food is nutrient deficient:

1. It is not real food. Most food people are costuming these days is processed rubbish with zero nutritional value.

2. Our farming methods suck. Hormones, fertilisers, intensive farming, etc… all these methods we have adopted to be more profitable are making our food less nutritious. I recently

Lazy health

read that an orange 50 years ago had the nutritional value of around 50 oranges in your standard supermarket today.

Our bodies understand what nutrition is needed to thrive and send the appropriate cues for you to fix any problem that may arise. If your body is missing nutrients it will send the signal that it is hungry so that you can get your ass off the sofa and get more food. And this is where it gets bad. More and more people go for the "easy" option of sugary and carb-rich food which quickly and conveniently fixes that problem for a very short amount of time. It fixes the short-term craving while creating a much larger one, your ass is actually getting larger.

I always strive to eliminate as much processed food as I possibly can and focus my diet on wild meat (at least grass-fed and grass-processed), unprocessed dairy and fruits. I feel more energised when my diet comprises only of these foods and I go above and beyond to make sure I don't deviate far from them. I don't beat myself up if I eat something else but I will make sure that if I do I make better choices for the next few days.

I am not telling you to replicate what I do, I just want you to find your happy place for your food intake and stick to it. The more simple your plan, the more likely you are to stick to it and succeed.

Lazy Happy Successful

Remember that science is not set in stone, it is an ever changing field with new data and conclusions being achieved regularly. This means that your diet choices should also adapt to new ideas and data. You should learn to listen to your body and eat whatever makes you feel more energised and alive while avoiding foods that make you feel like crap. A food diary is a great way to measure and quantify this. Take control over your food intake by measuring and adjusting it to suit your individual needs. It will not be an easy process but it is indispensable to your happiness and success.

Lazy money

Money is extremely important to our lazy philosophy because it leads to us regaining our time. If you don't have money you will have to spend very valuable time you could be using to create happiness into creating money instead.

The interesting thing about money is that it is not all the same.... there is active, and then there is passive money. Active money or income is when you trade your time for money. Passive money or income is when you let your money produce returns without your time input or with very little of it. Those returns can be in the form of income: like property rent, share dividends, crypto staking, etc...; or capital: like property equity growth, cryptocurrency value increases or appreciation in share value.

The name of the game is simple: replace your active income with passive income as quickly and safely as possible. If it seems easy, it is because it is easy. You just have to follow steps which are not comfortable but they do work. What is certain is that if you keep trading your time for money you will never truly enjoy and benefit from our philosophy. The reason for this is simple, our working conditions are inhumane and they make relaxation, fun and happiness practically impossible. So for this simple yet very powerful reason, you need to become a master at replacing your active income so you can truly be happy. I will discuss the four options you can use to create passive wealth because most people still don't get how you can do this in today's market.

The 4 lane motorway to passive wealth

I want to touch on the main aspects of each of the four main paths to creating passive wealth in today's market conditions. The four paths are:

    Real estate

    Business

    Shares

    Commodities

There is no right or wrong combination of them. You can use one or all. I would suggest you become an expert in at least two just in case the tide changes and you want to flow with the better performing asset class. What these four paths have in common is that they are all assets. My definition of an asset is something that when acquired produces income and increases in value over time. For example, your home is not an asset unless you rent part of it or derive an income through it in any other way. Buying something just because it should go up in value, like silver and gold, is speculation. For me gold and silver are therefore not assets, they are liabilities. I am not saying you should not have any speculative items in your portfolio, what I am saying is that you should only consider speculative items once your passive cash flow allows you to do so. Speculation has made me plenty of money so I will never put it down. The only concept I want to make sure you understand is that I want you to be safe first and foremost. The best way to keep you safe is by avoiding speculation until you can afford it.

Now that I have clarified these simple yet extremely important points let's dig a little deeper into the asset classes:

1. Real Estate

Real estate changed my life. I started buying properties in 2002 and have never looked back. I did a tremendous amount of research and focused on smaller, income producing properties with high yields and strong rental demand. I also made sure I focused on areas with serious infrastructure projects like new roads, hospitals, universities, etc... This meant that I could also accumulate wealth through capital appreciation. The play worked very well in the four different countries where I invested. I even breezed through the global financial crisis because I had discerned that my investments in Spain were too risky to maintain in late 2006, early 2007. The rest of my portfolio didn't even drop past 10% and recovered within 18 months to keep growing rapidly and healthily whilst producing income.

I love real estate for two main reasons:

Leverage. You can borrow money from lenders at higher percentages and lower interest in real estate than any other alternative. This is simply because real estate is considered the least risky of all the investment propositions. Leverage means that if I have $20,000 I can buy an asset valued at around $100,000 and make profits on the whole $100,000 rather than just my measly $20,000 invested. Essentially in this example, I am amplifying my returns times five by just using someone else's money. The problem with leverage is that it is a double edged sword. Besides amplifying profits it could also amplify losses. If you buy the wrong property and it goes down in value you will lose on the total value, not just your investment. This is why buying cashflow positive property is essential when you get started. If your property is producing cashflow you will very rarely be forced to sell it. If you are not forced to sell it and keep holding on to it for a longer time, you have not lost any money and properties historically will tend to rebound and grow anyways. So in this case you keep getting income while you wait for equity to build up. I always tell my seminar attendees this simple mantra: "the only time you can lose money through property investing is when you have to sell". Follow this mantra and your risk will be severely mitigated.

Its imperfect nature. Valuing a property is not a simple or exact science. There are too many variables to consider unless you are just dealing with box standard apartments in a development which are much easier to assess and price. This imperfect nature lends itself to giving the astute and educated investor an advantage. They can buy an asset under market value, and they can also add value to such asset through skilled renovation or change of use (subdivision, conversion, etc…). It is one of the two asset classes where you can make money when you buy! If that doesn't get your tail wagging I do not know what will….

There are many tips, pitfalls and strategies that I can't describe in this book. In my view, this is not what this book is all about. If you want to learn more about property investing and what it can do for you, I recommend you visit my website www.lazyhappysuccessful.com where you will find all you need to know to make better investment decisions in property and the rest of the asset classes.

2. Business

Maybe the hardest route of them all is business, because it usually involves trading a large chunk of your time and money until the business is profitable enough so you can replace yourself. By replacing yourself I mean hiring someone to take over your responsibilities so you can just be the non 1working owner. A business is usually valued following a simple formula: (profits x 2-7 depending on industry and location) + Assets + Goodwill (the potential for growth or to create extra revenue it may have).

What I love about business is that there are countless ways of increasing profits and for every dollar you increase in revenue you are also adding 2 to 7 dollars value into the business. For example, you bought a business for $350,000 (assume assets and goodwill at $50k of that price and an income multiple of 3) because the business was creating $100,000 of annual revenue. Over the next 24 months, you increase the revenue to $200,000 which is fantastic in itself since you doubled your income! Now not only you are making twice as much money but your business is worth $600,000!!! That is a $300,000 capital growth on your investment plus a $100,000 annual income growth.

Once again I need to reiterate that I only consider it a business if it continues to generate those annual returns without your input. I am okay with you being a part of the board of directors and making big decisions every few months, but it is not a business if you are running it or heavily involved.

3. Shares

Lazy money

Hopefully, you are not thinking of working on Wall Street or spending sleepless nights trading multiple shares in markets around the world. That is not investing, that is just another job and to me, JOB stands for Just Over Broke.

What I am proposing here is medium to long term transactions in shares in companies that will provide dividends (cashflow) and have growth potential. This is the most complex of all markets but at the same time the easiest one to set up. There is a plethora of options for all kinds of investors regardless of where you are, how much you know or how much money you have. There is even access to leverage (although I strongly encourage you to not use it until you have a lot of experience) and automation options. Most Western jurisdictions will also let you invest in the share market tax free directly from your income earned so you can accrue profits for your retirement. This is an avenue most income earners should explore but it lacks a basic and in my opinion the best benefit of investing in shares: Its liquidity.

Liquidity means that if you need money to buy something you can almost instantly sell your share position and transform it into cash to buy whatever you want. Real estate and businesses are not liquid markets and the transactions can take weeks, months or even years for complex business or real estate deals. This means that if you need that cash at short notice you should explore investing in shares as a powerful alternative.

4. Commodities

Commodities are natural products that are consumed by people and these products and their derivatives have been traded in open markets for a very long time. I consider precious metals like gold and silver a commodity, although, just like I explained before with your home, they are not assets since they do not produce income. Don't get me wrong, I own a fair amount of precious metals but it is a speculation play, not a safe investment in an asset.

Joining the commodities world is the vast universe of cryptocurrency powered by the best and most robust ledger ever: the blockchain. Crypto does meet the asset definition as it can produce income if you stake it and it can go up in price. To me, the blockchain looks and feels a lot like when the internet first came into play. It is a game changer and we are at the initial adoption stage still.

As governments stumble to find solutions to the financial crisis they have created through their senseless and futile mandates to curve the spread of Covid 19, they will all start creating their digital cryptocurrencies (CBDCs) as their traditional currencies lose value in the inflationary world they have created. This will signify the end of the early adoption phase and the beginning of the mass adoption period.

My prediction is that NFTs (Non Fungible Tokens) will become comparable to our current websites which will be supported by the blockchain as the internet supports our current websites. NFTs will act as electronic receipts for everything from art to consumer items. This will revolutionise the way we do business and transact in general. If you are not learning about this new technology, you will regret it in just a few years time when you will have to use it whether you want it or not. Once again you can visit www.lazyhappysuccessful.com for more information and education on crypto assets and technology.

I will also give you one of the best tips ever when it comes to creating wealth. If you want bigger paychecks you have to solve bigger problems. Think about it. The people that solve the biggest problems will always get paid more than the ones who solve the little ones.

Hormonal cycles affect your investment decisions

Just like I explained in the Lazy Health section hormones also affect your financial decisions. When I look back at some of my best business deals they tend to have come to fruition in after work meetings (between 6 pm - 10 pm) or during long lunches (the longer the better). I now very rarely schedule any calls or meetings in the morning and dedicate that prime testosterone time to health and achievement. This is when I get shit done. Calls and meetings are a thing to do around lunch or evenings. I am ruthless when it comes to calls and meetings and will not do them unless I am certain there is a benefit to them. There is nothing more frustrating for me than to meet someone for an hour or so to achieve what could have been achieved in a 5 minute email or call. Business meetings are for big decision making and to strengthen relationships, that is it.

You can also "hack" your testosterone level if you know you are going to need it for a short amount of time at an inconvenient time. It is scientifically proven that you will increase your testosterone level (momentarily but long enough to impact an activity) if you exercise vigorously, get sexually aroused (do or watch whatever rocks your boat but do not ejaculate!!!), watch your favourite team win (watching your favourite team lose will deplete your testosterone) or have a short nap.

You need to listen to your body in a world where people have lost that connection and try to perform their revenue making activities like robots. You will achieve more and have a more balanced and happier life if you reconnect with your own body and start making better decisions at better times.

Obviously, your hormonal balance also changes throughout your life. This affects how we perceive the world and our own decision making. Some years of your life will be better suited for specific activities while others will feel like you are rowing against an extremely strong current. The key to this fact is to be patient and to use your strengths at the right time. Remember TAG, think, act, get.

Always a learner

You have to keep on top of new ideas and developments when it comes to investing in any assets. If you have the mentality of a student, you will be able to foresee and adapt to new paradigms and profit handsomely while at it.

Learning is fun anyways, so make sure you get your fair share of it.

Understanding ROI and ROTI

I want to conclude this section by talking about the most powerful formula and concept when analysing any form of investment.

R.O.I. (Return On Investment)

R.O.T.I. (Return On Time Invested)

R.O.I. = Profit / Cash Invested (usually expressed as a percentage)

R.O.T.I. = Profit / Hours of time invested

Lazy Happy Successful

Your goal is to maximise R.O.I. and R.O.T.I. until you get infinite returns in both! You may ask, how do you do that …. well, the mathematical answer is simple: Invest none of your money and time.

For example, Elon Musk recently purchased Twitter. Elon is the richest man on the planet but instead of using his money, he announced that he was going to use finance and other people's money to settle the purchase. Why would the richest man in the world use someone else's money rather than his own? Because he understands R.O.I. and what it takes to be wealthy.

The theory is simple then, but what about the practical aspect of these formulae? I can tell you that it is also simple but it takes two special skills to be applied:

1. Experience

2. Strategic clarity

In terms of experience, it can be your own or you can "borrow" it through education or coaching. Investors who will provide you with the funds for your investment will need to believe in you before they let go of their funds. To me, it is also very logical to borrow someone else's experience rather than use yours. I hate wasting time and making mistakes and working with people that have already made them will save you both time and painful headaches.

Lazy money

Strategic clarity has two subcomponents.

You need to have clarity and believe in your strategy without any doubt or hesitation. That means that you are the expert on the investment.

But that is not enough, you also need to be able to convey that clarity to investors and that is where most wannabe entrepreneurs fail miserably. If you have ever watched the tv program "Shark Tank" you understand exactly what I mean by this. Most entrepreneurs that go to the sharks (investors) asking for funding don't have the ability to portray trust and knowledge and that is why they fail to secure investment funds. It is not so much the product or business idea, it is their lack of clarity and communication skills.

The reality about minimising risk and time to create wealth is that it is much easier to achieve when you work with the right people and invest enough quality time to become an expert in an area. Surround yourself with the right tribe to maximise performance. My last piece of advice for you is to go out there and make it happen. The quicker you get to your financial goals the more life you will have to truly enjoy happiness, whatever happiness means to you.

www.ingramcontent.com/pod-product-compliance
Lightning Source LLC
Chambersburg PA
CBHW021102080526
44587CB00010B/342